"There once was a nation of 200 million people that was the most powerful country in all the world. . . . Seventy per cent of the population was crowded into 1 per cent of the land, which they called cities. . . . The basic trouble, said the wise men, is not how badly people move, but how bleakly they live. What we need is trees and grass and fresh air, decent houses and schools, and convenient recreation. People should spend their time enjoying the city instead of spending their money escaping it. . . ."

—from *A Fable of American Cities*
by Wilfred Owen

The City as a Community revolves around the theme that man created cities for a better way of life; now he must use his ingenuity to keep the cities from destroying himself and the good life.

PROBLEMS OF AMERICAN SOCIETY

Focusing on the urban scene, youth, the individual and his search for a better life, the books in this series probe the most crucial dilemmas of our time.

The Negro in the City
Civil Rights and Civil Liberties
Crime and Juvenile Delinquency
Poverty and the Poor
Air and Water Pollution
The Traffic Jam
The Slums
The Draft
The City as a Community
The Consumer
Drugs
Riots
Minorities All
Governing the City
Hunger
Prisons
Racism
Police

GERALD LEINWAND

assisted by
Richard E. Scheetz

The City as a Community

PUBLISHED BY POCKET BOOKS NEW YORK

THE CITY AS A COMMUNITY

A POCKET BOOK edition
1st printing.........March, 1970

The City as a Community was originally published under the
imprint of WASHINGTON SQUARE PRESS, a division of
Simon & Schuster, Inc.

This original POCKET BOOK edition is printed from
brand-new plates made from newly set, clear, easy-to-read type.
POCKET BOOK editions are published by POCKET BOOKS, a division of
Simon & Schuster, Inc., 630 Fifth Avenue, New York, N.Y. 10020.
Trademarks registered in the United States and other countries.

L

5654

To my parents
who taught me to live
in urban America

ACKNOWLEDGMENT

This is one of a series of volumes designed to become text materials for urban schools. Partially funded under Title I, Elementary and Secondary Education Act, Public Law 89–10, 1965, the series grew out of a curriculum development project conceived and executed by the editor. Washington Square Press and the Curriculum Committee of the Trenton, New Jersey, public schools provided valuable editorial assistance.

Mrs. Bernice Munce is Project Supervisor of the Curriculum Committee which includes the following members: William Carter, Elsie Collins, Albert De-Martin, Harold P. DuShane, Barbara Hancock, Roland Hence, Steven McLaine, Gerald Popkin, Richard Scheetz, Carol West.

Also contributing to the effort were Neil O'Donnel, Joseph Fonseca and Eugene Winchester as research assistants, Mrs. Eileen Donohue as secretary, and my wife who spent hours typing and proofreading.

The opera at Lincoln Center in New York City provides some of the finest entertainment in the city. (Joe Molnar)

Preface

It is an axiom of Euclidean geometry that the whole is equal to the sum of its parts. In the case of a city, however, even an introductory study such as this one must come to grips with the fact that the organic city is greater than the sum of its parts. A city is not merely a concentration of people. It is not merely an industrial, cultural, and economic center. It is not only the business and residential sections of which it is composed. A city to be sure is all of these, but the city is more. It is a community in which all aspects of life are drawn together in hopes of creating a desirable way of life for its inhabitants. Defining a city is no easy task. Indicating the nature of the community out of which a city grows and which it in turn creates is more difficult still. The character of life in megalopolitan America, that is, in the northeastern portion of the country, provides a foretaste of things to come and points to new directions for the organization of the institutions of American society.

As do other volumes in this series, this book begins with a brief overview of the character of city life and how it came to be what it is. It attempts an interdisciplinary approach since the study is neither exclusively historical, economic, sociological, nor anthropological. Yet it draws on each of these disciplines even if in only an elementary way. In approaching the city as a community in this way, it is not especially necessary to identify the separate disciplines upon which the study draws. It is enough if readers come away with the idea that the city is the dynamic element in American life today and that many of the problems of urban life grow out of the fact that the nation has just become aware of it. Because of the persistence of the "rural myth," many of our political, economic, and social institutions are out of balance with this decisive force in our affairs.

Following the essay are fifteen selected, annotated readings designed to identify various facets of the city as a community. The first group of readings presents general principles and problems associated with urban life. The second group of readings provides descriptions of selected world cities; it is hoped that these readings not only will have intrinsic interest and arouse a sense of awe in the reader for what the city is and what it is likely to become, but also that they will indicate how men, at various times, were impressed with what they saw on their visits to some of the world's great cities.

The essay and the readings that follow will not provide solutions for the contradictions in urban life. Instead, it is hoped that they will raise questions and that these questions will encourage further reading. This is an introductory study only and as such is no more than a bare beginning of an examination of a web of complex problems, which the city as a community must solve if the city is to provide a climate for the healthful growth of mankind.

G. L.

Contents

PREFACE

PART ONE:

The Problem and the Challenge

What Is a City? ... 17
Why Is the City a Community? ... 24
How Did Cities Get Their Start? ... 27
What Is the Lure of the City? ... 34
What Is the Difference between Urban
   and Rural? ... 40
Who Are the People of the City? ... 45
Why Are People Leaving the City? ... 46
Has the Movement to the Suburbs Helped
   or Hurt the Central City? ... 52
Did the Middle Class Find What They Wanted
   in the Suburb? ... 54
How May Cities Be More Effectively
   Planned? ... 57
What Is the Future of the City? ... 61

PART TWO:

Selected Readings

1. *What Is a Town?*
   by EMRYS JONES ... 69

2. *Country, Suburb, City*
   by DOROTHY BARCLAY ... 73

Contents

3. *The Lure of the City*
   by BLAKE MCKELVEY   79

4. *The Urban Problem*
   by RAYMOND VERNON   84

5. *Main Street of the Nation*
   by WOLF VON ECKARDT   90

6. *A Fable of American Cities*
   by WILFRED OWEN   100

7. *The Uses of City Neighborhoods*
   by JANE JACOBS   111

8. *The Coming Era of Ecumenopolis*
   by C. A. DOXIADIS   121

9. *Ancient Babylon*
   by HERODOTUS   131

10. *Mexico City in Montezuma's Time*
    by HERNANDO CORTES   135

11. *Chicago—The Young Giant*
    by W. E. WOODWARD   141

12. *New Orleans in the 1880's*
    by MARK TWAIN   149

13. *Tokyo, in the 1950's*
    by FOSCO MARAINI   157

14. *Brasilia*
    by JOHN DOS PASSOS   163

15. *Reston, Virginia: A New Town*
    by ERVIN GALANTAY   168

Footnotes   177
Index   181

Part One

The Problem and the Challenge

ARISTOTLE, a famous philosopher of ancient Greece, wrote, "Men come together in cities to live. They remain to live the good life."[1] But does one in fact find the good life in the city? How well are the needs for the good life being met? What are those needs? And what is the good life insofar as urban living is concerned?

Surely the good life requires many things. The good life in the city requires pure water, fresh air, rapid and inexpensive transit, efficient law enforcement, and fire protection. The good life also requires effective collection of garbage, proper disposal of sewage, and provision for good housing for all the people of the city. In talking about the good life in the city one cannot limit oneself merely to the things we can see, feel, and touch. The urban good life requires other things as well. It requires that the city make provision for jobs for its people. It requires that the city provide for the education of its children and its adults. The urban good life requires that the people have libraries and museums to which they may go. There must be places for wholesome recreation and amusement in parks and in playgrounds. There must be provision for concerts and for plays which are inexpensive to attend and available to all. The good life requires that there be

America's mobile population first settled in farm areas, but for the last century they have been moving to urban areas. (Reprinted from *U.S. News & World Report,* November 6, 1967. Copyright © 1967 by *U.S. News & World Report*)

adequate care for the sick and for the poor. And the good life in the city requires that its government be democratically chosen and efficiently run.

Seven out of ten Americans presently live in cities. Hence, when one discusses the "good life" of the city one is really discussing what it takes for most Americans to be able to live well. The riots that occurred during the summer of 1967 may well be taken as evidence that, despite what Aristotle said, too many urban people are not living well at all. If this is so, why did people come to the city in the first place? Why do cities continue to grow? Why are they located where they are? These are some of the questions we will try to answer. Few answers are more urgently needed. "Human beings have congregated in cities for more than 50 centuries, but

Some people never get to know what the "good life" means. Young children living in slum housing are the group most seriously affected. (Fletcher Drake-OEO)

it took only two to bring the cities of the United States into a state of serious crisis."[2] In trying to find out more about the crises of the cities of the twentieth century, we will find out what cities were like many years ago and what they might be like in the future.

What Is a City?

A city may be defined in many ways. One way to define it is to say that it is a unit of government which has been created by the state. Usually it has a large concentration of people, but mere numbers are not enough of a guide to a definition of a city.

The Lower East Side of New York City in 1898, showing that in the nineteenth century a neighborhood was a place to live, work, and socialize. (The Byron Collection— Museum of the City of New York)

In Kansas, a community with as few as two hundred people may become a city. And Vergennes, a city in rural western Vermont, has a population of less than two thousand, yet it too is a city. The United States census classifies as cities all incorporated communities with 2,500 or more people. An incorporated community is one that has special powers to tax and spend its money and govern itself. While it is possible to define a city politically by saying that it must have a certain number of people and occupy certain political boundaries, such a definition does not give us an insight into the dynamic, living qualities a city has.

Because of such qualities it is easier to talk about a city than to say what it is. When, as in medieval days, cities had walls around them, the city consisted of those people who lived within its walls. When, during the nineteenth century, people sought to live close to their place of business or employment, the business district and the area immediately surrounding it was the city. A striking example of the latter is London, England. The original city of London proper is about a square mile in size, and in this area there may be found the commercial and financial heart of Britain, including the Bank of England and a host of important financial and business enterprises. The City of London was first recognized by Queen Elizabeth I during the sixteenth century. Since that time greater London has grown and expanded far beyond its original boundaries.

The expansion of cities beyond the immediate "downtown" area, or hub, as it may be called, has been going on for many years. New York City, for example, expanded far beyond its financial core situated at Broad and Wall streets. Similarly, Chicago grew out well beyond its "downtown" area, known the world over as "the Loop." The kind of expansion that took place depended largely on the means of transportation available to the people. The age of the steam locomotive, for example, speeded the shipping of goods and the movement of people into the core of the city. It made it possible for goods to move out of the city to other cities. But it did little to improve getting around within the city itself, since the steam engine was not appro-

Typical slum dwellings in Atlanta, Georgia. The toilet facilities serve all the occupants of this building, which is divided into eight housekeeping units. (Wide World)

priate for city traffic. The steam locomotive tended to encourage the further concentration of people around a city's financial district, railroad terminal, and harbor. Houses were built so close together that there came to be no space between them. Row houses, as these are called, usually run down, and now perhaps housing stores as well as people, are still a characteristic feature of the central city.

When the streetcar was introduced, it became

The San Francisco Freeway is typical of the highways that divide and ring all of our major cities. (American Airlines)

possible for people to live farther away from the central city than they had before. People went "downtown" by streetcar and later by elevated train and subway, which were convenient and relatively inexpensive means of transportation. Up to 1910, the traditional core of the city was still its most important business center. However, with the coming of the automobile all this was changed.

Because of the automobile, people could live farther away from the downtown area than ever before. While the very rich who could afford to live luxuriously in the downtown areas stayed, the prosperous middle class began to move to the outskirts of the city. The poor, unable to move, and too poor to afford an automobile, remained behind. The core of most large cities today tends to be made up of the traditional business areas, the homes and apartments of the very rich, and the slums of the very poor. Because the prosperous middle class was moving out of the city, business tended to follow. Large stores and banks opened branches, and small stores found a new population to serve. The city became ringed with highways. The old pattern of movement of people and goods changed radically, and again the precise shape and size of the city became difficult to determine. The city is more than the downtown area; it is more than the people who live near the central business district. But if it is more than the people who live in it, what is a city?

Another way to define a city may be the following: A city is ". . . any large concentration of people with a differentiation of economic functions."[3] As we have already noted, however, a city need not be a large concentration of people. And, in any event, there is uncertainty as to how many people

Although cities are thought of as being cold and impersonal, scenes like this of people meeting and enjoying a conversation are taking place every day. (Bill Anderson-Monkmeyer)

living in one place will make up such a concentration. But this definition introduces a new idea, namely the idea of a city as a community in which those tasks that make a city flourish, prosper, and grow depend upon the people who live there and the kind of community they build.

Why Is the City a Community?

If you have read the story of Robinson Crusoe you will remember that he had been marooned on what seemed to be a deserted island. The story describes not only his adventures but how he built a raft and a house, obtained food, and, with articles he had been able to salvage from the wrecked ship, was able to live for eighteen years in relative comfort but entirely alone. Finally, Robinson Crusoe discovered a man on the island who had escaped from cannibals. Friday, as this man was called, became both a servant and a friend to Robinson Crusoe, and the two were able to establish what neither of them alone could have done—a simple community.

A community may be described as a group of people who come together to live in a particular area because they have something in common. Crusoe and Friday wanted each other's company. They both needed protection from the cannibals who had tried to kill Friday. Both required the common necessities of life that together they could provide more easily.

There are many kinds of communities. The neighborhood is a community. The school is a community with common interests and rules for all its members. The nation itself is a community, as is the world. All men, wherever they live, have similar

The city can be a lonely place for people of all ages. (Joe Molnar)

needs for food, clothing, shelter. They have hopes for a better life for themselves and high hopes for their children. Just as modern industry and technology made the city community possible, so too have they made a world community possible. The jet plane, the telephone, the telegraph, and TV communication via satellite have drawn the countries of the world close together. Problems of overpopulation and of housing and of poverty are all problems that the world community faces. They probably cannot be solved without the collective effort of that community.

The city as a community is the focus of our concern. In this city community people live and work together for common purposes, even though they may not always realize they are doing this. Each person in a city depends upon another person in the city for his welfare and comfort. He relies on the police to protect him against crime. He relies on the fire department to protect him against fire. But each person has many more relationships in the city. He depends upon others for his job or he provides jobs for others. The work in the city is specialized. The city person looks to the milkman to deliver his milk, to the bank teller to take his money, to the repairman to fix his television set, and to the automobile mechanic to repair his car.

In rural areas the community is somewhat different. There is probably less specialization. Each person tends to know everybody else in the community. The TV repairman and the milkman are friends and neighbors. They do more than perform a specific service. Relationships with such people become friendly and social. In the city, one knows very few people. Indeed, because there are so many, on the one hand it is physically impossible to know all, and on the other, one must make a choice of those people whom he wishes to know well. It is for this reason that the city has developed a reputation for "not caring," of being indifferent to the individual.

In a certain sense this is true. We in the city know less about our neighbors than do those who live in small towns. But our neighbors know less about us as well. This anonymity frees us to think and do what we wish and to go where we like. There is a greater amount of privacy in the city, and the additional freedom that goes with it. The city is a different sort of community than that found in the country, with different attractions and opportunities. It is not so much an impersonal place in which to live as it is a place where men may more readily be able to live as they wish. Because it has fostered this kind of community, the city has had an important role in the rise of civilization.

How Did Cities Get Their Start?

Before there were nations there were cities. The city existed as the hub of everything man did. The very center of the Roman empire was the city of Rome. And Greece was not a nation at all, but a group of independent, city-centered communities. These cities, or city-states as they are called, had powers that the city in which you live today does not possess. For example, the city of Athens had the power to make war and agree to treaties of peace. It had the power to coin money and to grant or withhold citizenship. Thus, in ancient Greece, men were Athenians or Corinthians or Thebans rather than "Greeks."

It is not too much to say that the story of cities is the story of civilized man. Indeed, the very word

"civilization" comes from the Latin word for city
(civitas), as does the word "citizen." Citizens were
the property owners and the taxpayers of a city,
and upon them the city depended for survival. Often
those in the lower classes and those who had been
conquered were denied the privileges that went with
citizenship. Such privileges included choosing partic-
ipants in government or taking part in government
oneself if one wished. The origins of cities go back
to the very dawn of civilization; still, if the total
length of time man has been on earth is likened to
a clock, with twelve o'clock representing the present, then the time at which man began to form
cities can be represented as but a minute before
twelve.

The first settled communities began to appear in
the river valleys of the Tigris and the Euphrates in
ancient Mesopotamia, of the Nile in ancient Egypt,
and of the Ganges in India and the Yangtze in
China. In these areas men learned at an early date
to grow food and to make animals useful to them in
farming. They learned to plant seeds and to culti-
vate the land. When men had mastered these skills,
they did not have to spend their days wandering
about in search of food. They could then live in
established communities. These communities grew as
men gathered together to work and to seek protection against common enemies. Some of these early
communities became the first cities.

In his book *The Culture of Cities,*[4] Lewis Mumford shows the rise of a city, which began simply
as a gathering place and later—as in the case of the
medieval cities of Europe (roughly between 500 and
1200 A.D.)—became a fortress with heavy walls
and a moat surrounding it for protection. Later still,
the city became an industrial center, a place where

men might buy and sell manufactured goods. Cities have always developed as the result of some technical advance. Thus the first cities were made possible by the fact that man learned to farm and so could live in settled communities. Cities continued to grow because the use of farm machinery made it possible for relatively few farmers to feed many people, and those who were not needed on the farm went to live in the city. Improved means of transportation and communication allowed people to live more easily in cities by keeping them in touch with other cities and by making goods from distant farms and factories easily available.

Cities grew in their own right as they became focal points for the buying, selling, and shipping of goods. Chicago and Kansas City became centers for the slaughter and packing of cattle from Texas. Pittsburgh flourished because of its booming iron and steel industry. Many of the cities of New England owe their development to the textile and shoe industries, while Detroit grew up along with the manufacture of the automobile. Miami and Las Vegas became entertainment capitals of the world, while Los Angeles became the motion picture center of America. As Max Lerner remarked, "At some point in its history every American city has been a 'boom' city. . . ."[5] That is, every city at one time or another provided, or seemed to provide, an unusual opportunity for people to get rich quickly, to get better jobs, or to bring up their families in more luxurious ways. The Gold Rush of 1849 helped San Francisco grow; while the great Florida land boom of the 1920s contributed to the development of Miami. Silver, oil, and, later, the movies were responsible for the rise of Los Angeles.

Unlike European cities, the cities of America grew

very quickly. Yet on both continents the city has always occupied a special place in the minds and hearts of men. During the medieval period, when many men were serfs and worked on the land of a feudal lord for the bare necessities of life, there was a saying that "city air makes one free." This saying had much truth to it. For one thing, if a serf could escape to the city and live there for a year or so, he was no longer a serf, but attained automatically the status of free man. The rise of cities was therefore opposed by the feudal lords, who saw in the hustle and bustle of the city a challenge to their society in which there was a place for every man and where everyone was in his place. Today, although living in a city no longer makes one free in the legal sense, the city, with its many opportunities for cultural and personal enrichment, continues to hold out a promise of freedom, and that promise holds as great an attraction as it has since earliest times.

Cities grew up where men were accustomed to gather. Thus, in both ancient and modern times, they have been founded on the banks of rivers. The place where a river empties out into an ocean to form a harbor—as the Hudson does in New York —becomes the geographically natural location for a city. Ships from faraway places can bring their goods and passengers into the harbor, and merchants from the interior may come into the city with the goods and farm products they wish to sell. Pittsburgh is located on the banks of the Allegheny and the Monongahela, where they form the mighty Ohio; the capital of the nation is situated at the head of the Potomac. New Orleans is the city at the mouth of the Mississippi, where it empties into the Gulf of Mexico. St. Louis owes its beginning

Many of our cities grew up along the banks of rivers or in areas that had good harbors. Stevedores still play an active role in our port cities. (Jack Eisenberg-OEO)

to the pioneers of old who gathered there to buy their necessities and weapons and to organize themselves for the long trek to homesteads beyond the Mississippi. An arch set on the bank of the Mississippi marks the symbolic point of departure of the covered wagons from St. Louis on their way west.

Early American communities were scattered all down the east coast and along its rivers. Many early American cities were established on the "fall line." Although waterfalls interfered with navigation and transportation along our eastern rivers and forced men to carry their goods around them, the falls also produced the mechanical power needed to turn the first mills, and on sites along the fall line grew cities like Raleigh and Columbia, North Carolina; Baltimore; Philadelphia; and Trenton.

Other cities began because some other important natural resource was nearby. Many mining towns grew up around the Great Lakes: Duluth, Minnesota, for example, is not only an important terminus on Lake Superior but is near the iron ore deposits of the Mesabi Range. Butte, Montana, was a silver-mining town, while many of the cities of the Pacific Northwest owe their start to the lumbering resources in the vicinity.

Just as cities get their start from the favoring geographic factors that make their growth possible and from the resources that are nearby, so men also have an effect on where cities are located. The building of railroads across the country made possible the growth of some cities like St. Louis and Chicago, which became great railroad terminals. And in those places where cattle trails met the railroad towns there grew the cities of western fame, like Abilene, Cheyenne, and Dodge City. During America's early days few developments, however, were as important in giving cities their start as the Erie Canal. Not only did it give a spurt to the growth of New York City itself, but it made the growth of Albany and Buffalo possible, to say nothing of cities like Utica and Rochester, which were along its route. The building of the Erie Canal connected the Great Lakes with the eastern coast and contributed to the growth of cities as far west as Cleveland, Chicago, and Detroit.

It has been said of the city that "it is a fact in nature, like a cave, or a run of mackerel, or an

This folk singer in a Greenwich Village café entertains audiences of tourists and natives alike. (Sam Faulk-Monkmeyer)

ant-heap."[6] According to this view, men did not consciously form cities. Instead, men, simply because they were men, had to live together, work together, create art and music together. Men could not live alone even if they wanted to. But, once formed, the city has a way of molding men as well. ". . . Urban forms condition mind."[7] That is, the city makes men something they were not. For this reason, men have long been suspicious of the city, feeling that the city was making them worse rather than better. It was on the farm and in the joys of rural life that the good life, and good men, were to be found. Yet it was in search of the good life that men, almost without willing it, built cities, and from cities—at least as often as from farms—great men have risen.

What Is the Lure of the City?

Cities grow mainly because people are attracted to them. If cities depended for growth upon a natural increase due to the birth of children within their boundaries, that growth would be very slow indeed. As a matter of fact, birth rates in cities are likely to be lower than those in the country, and families in cities tend to be smaller than those in the country. Most large cities grow because they lure immigrants from foreign nations, or in-migrants from farms in this country. The growth of every large city in the United States is the result mainly of attractions that the city holds and of the expectations of people who come to it.

The cities of America have drawn people to them from early colonial days. While fewer than 10 percent of the early Americans lived in what may be called cities, these communities acted like a magnetic force in pulling people off the farm and bringing them to the city. Young men, disappointed with farming, looked for excitement and adventure. They turned to the city to fulfill their dreams. They hired out on ships or served apprenticeships to silversmiths, gunsmiths, shopkeepers, or merchants; in this way they could provide their own food, shelter, and clothing.

The country also propelled some people toward the city. The task of living off the land was a difficult and at times an impossible one. From dawn to dusk the farmer cared for his land and hunted for meat for his family. The wife cooked, kept house, made the clothing, and was even responsible for

These jobless migrant workers standing in a bread line in Florida remind us of the depression of the 1930's. Migrant farm workers are not only the lowest-paid group in our labor force, but many times during the year they have no work at all. (Wide World)

providing some of the luxuries, such as soap, candles, and, on occasion, ice cream.

As difficult as this life was, it became worse if the soil was poor or if the year was dry and the crops were small. For this reason some young men and entire families moved to the city. There the head of the family might take up a trade to provide the necessities of life for his family. In the process he could spend more time with his family than he had on the farm.

Yankee Doodle came to town
Riding on a pony,
Stuck a feather in his hat
And called it macaroni.
Yankee Doodle, keep it up,
Yankee Doodle dandy
Mind the music and the step
And with the girls be handy.[8]

This early American tune, first sung by the British to make fun of the colonists during the Revolutionary War, also tells the story of the farm youth who comes to town. It shows the contempt the city dwellers had for the country boy, whom they called "Yankee Doodle." Many farmers shunned the city, believing it to be a sinful place. Still, as the song says, our Yankee Doodle friend did come to town, and the lure of the city continued to grow.

Here in the City I ponder,
Through its long pathways I wander.
These are the spires that are gleaming,
All through my juvenile dreaming.[9]

This poem is entitled "Wealth." It was written about a hundred years after "Yankee Doodle." It shows that during the nineteenth century youth would continue to look for riches or wealth in the city. The city at that time was also taking on a new look. While it was constantly growing outward, it was also growing upward. The "spires" in the poem suggest this fact. The industrial progress of the last twenty-five years of the nineteenth century gave cities the appearance that they have to this day. Steel made skyscrapers possible. Trolley lines were extended, and the subway and even the automobile

Large numbers of Jews came from Eastern Europe from 1890 to 1920 and settled in large cities, especially in the Lower East Side of New York City. (New York Public Library Picture Collection)

were not far in the future. New industry developed in textiles and in printing, in shops and factories. And labor was desperately needed to do the work required.

While the country and the farm supplied the city

with some workers, there were still not enough, and many immigrants came from Europe to fill this need. Germans, Irish, Italians, Scandinavians, and Jews are just a few of the groups represented. Japanese and Chinese also came to find work, which was plentiful in the city. This great influx of people continued through the late nineteenth into the early twentieth century.

During the twentieth century two additional groups moved in ever-increasing numbers to the cities of the North. During World Wars I and II, when many men were overseas, job opportunities in the North attracted many southern Negroes to northern urban centers. Negroes also came hoping to find a better life than that which existed for them in the South. After World War II, Puerto Ricans began to move to northern cities. Like the Negroes, they sought such jobs as might be found in the city. Many of these jobs were poorly paid and required few skills. Both Negroes and Puerto Ricans replaced the earlier immigrants in seeking jobs that were at the lowest end of the pay scale. However, as further industrial advances did away with the need for many unskilled jobs, living in the city was a real hardship for both groups. Lacking as they did adequate education, they found jobs on higher levels difficult, if not impossible, to obtain. Yet, despite these very real hardships, the city still appeared to hold out a promise that the country could not possibly offer.

Max Lerner in *America as a Civilization* suggests that "comfort, opportunity, glamour"[10] were the three main reasons for the attraction of the city and for its growth. Comfort was especially important for American women ". . . who found the frontier settlements bleak and welcomed the restoration of Eu-

Strolling through art galleries is a favorite pastime in the city. (The Museum of Modern Art, New York)

ropean comfort to the American situation."[11] In addition to comfort, which frontier life could scarcely begin to afford, there was the idea of the city as a glamorous place in which to live. Young men and women were drawn to the city because there they were allowed greater freedom in dress and in living. It was in the city that they found the more exciting writers and artists. The city had a greater choice of people and thus there were better opportunities to find love and to marry. But probably the greatest lure was the real or imagined opportunity which the city seemed to hold. "Often the mass city proved to be a jungle in which many were destroyed. . . . But those who build a temple to the idols of success do not inquire too closely about the burdens of the sacrifices."[12]

What Is the Difference between Urban and Rural?

Take a drive from Boston or New York City to Washington, D.C. You will find that you are scarcely out of one city before you are approaching the outskirts of the other. So densely populated has this northeastern region become that a new word has had to be found for it and for regions like it. The "megalopolis" (from the Greek, meaning "big city"), the area that extends from the east coast of Massachusetts down to Virginia, covers about four hundred miles and includes over 35 million people. It has been described as the "Main Street of the Nation."[13] Main Street in the city was the business center, where farmers and city dwellers bought and sold goods. On a greater scale, the megalopolis is the center for much of the business conducted in the United States and indeed in the world as well. While the megalopolis of the eastern seaboard is now the nation's greatest, there are others in the making—for example, the areas around Chicago, Detroit, and San Francisco. Such growth have cities had that they spill over their original boundaries. They embrace many different kinds of government, people, and industry. In a real sense, the difference between urban and rural has been all but lost.

When we use the term "urban," we mean it to describe those people who live in or near cities and who earn their living in business or industry. The "rural" population lives on the farms, and the people earn their living through farming. The movement of people from rural areas into the central parts of the city may be thought of as the process of urbanization. An urban area, however, comprises not only the central city, but the area surrounding it as well. Thus, Nassau and Westchester Counties, while not

This new slum clearance project contributes to the "urban sprawl" of the city. (Wide World)

in New York City itself, nevertheless are part of the urban area. The suburbs, as those areas which border the cities of any size are called, have become more attractive as the automobile has made it possible for people to live on the outskirts of the city and to drive in relative comfort to work. Where easy transit to the central city permits, some people move even farther away, into the so-called exurbs. The movement of people from the central city to any of the suburbs or exurbs of the great cities of America is another aspect of the process of urbanization. Thus urbanization must be thought of as the movement of people not only from rural areas to the city, but from the city to the suburbs and exurbs as well. In a real sense, once a man's family moves into the suburbs, while he may have left the city, he rarely stops living the urban life. Thus, the peo-

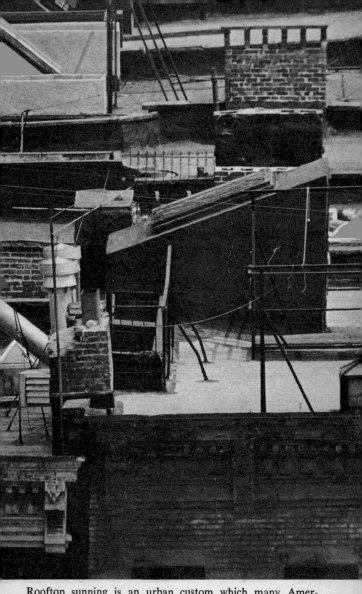

Rooftop sunning is an urban custom which many Americans might find unappealing. (Sam Faulk-Monkmeyer)

ple who live in suburban areas are mainly urban
people who work in urban industry and have
chosen not to live in the central city. As a result
of "urban sprawl," as the spreading out of the city
into the suburbs has been called, some of our central cities are actually declining in population. The
surrounding suburbs, on the other hand, continue
to grow rapidly.

The suburbs together with the city proper may be
called the metropolitan area. These areas spill over
into other states as well. For example, the New York
Metropolitan Region is made up of twenty-two
counties: Nine of these are in New Jersey, twelve
are in New York, and one is in Connecticut. A large
city, Newark, is actually in the New York Metropolitan Region. It should be noted that each metropolitan area includes the government of the big city—
whether it be New York, Chicago, San Francisco,
Philadelphia, or Detroit—and all the governments
of towns, villages, counties, and townships in the
area. In the United States today, according to the
Bureau of the Census, there are 225 metropolitan
areas of 50,000 population or more. These metropolitan areas may be expected to grow rapidly. "In
the next twenty years," it is believed, "we will add
54,000,000 people to these same metropolitan areas
—the equivalent of adding enough people to fill
five New Yorks or twenty-seven Washingtons."[14] It
is true that America has become, ". . . to a greater
extent than before, a nation of suburban and exurban
towns and villages,"[15] and American life is predominantly metropolitan in nature.

Although the city as a central area which is easily
identifiable geographically is declining, its influence
is growing over wider and wider areas. While the
number of people living in the city's hub may be

getting smaller, the influence of the city is becoming greater. The dominant influence in American life today is the city which really reaches out into and leaves its impression upon the country. When our nation was young, farming was dominant and agriculture influenced the way Americans lived. Today, the opposite is true. One of the basic problems in America today is how to adjust its politics, its economy, and its people to the fact that we have become a nation dominated by an urban way of life.

Who Are the People of the City?

"In its layout the city tends to reflect the life history of its movement of immigrants."[16] That is, in the residential pattern of every city may be seen the evidence of successive waves of immigration. Kielbasa is featured in markets in a Polish neighborhood; gefilte fish will be found in stores in a Jewish area. Bodegas serve the Spanish-speaking residents. Local radio stations may carry broadcasts in foreign tongues. And the market for foreign language newspapers may likewise be a large one. Each neighborhood, such as Chinatown or Little Italy, becomes a ghetto sheltering the people of a particular national or religious group. The culture and the customs of the group are preserved in these areas, thus giving the city its varied and colorful life. Thus, as darkness falls on Friday the hush of the approaching Sabbath descends on some of the Orthodox Jewish sections of Brooklyn; Little Italy enjoys a feast which lasts several days, to observe the traditions of its patron saint; and Chinatown draws crowds of visitors when it exuberantly celebrates the Chinese New Year.

These immigrant ghettos served a useful function.

They made it easier for the newly arrived immigrant to adjust gradually to America. Here he could find others who spoke his own language, and those who would help him find shelter and get a job. In the ghetto he could cling to his traditions without ridicule and he could at least try to bring up his children according to the traditions of his people. But the ghetto also had serious shortcomings. Ghettos were often marked by overcrowding, and these areas became essentially slums. Here poverty, disease, crime, and delinquency existed. And here too was violence, which often pitted one immigrant group against another.

Since the 1920s, when laws reduced to a trickle the flow of European immigrants, the pattern of city life changed. The original immigrants, who left their mark on the city, have now been followed in most large cities by in-migrants from Puerto Rico and by Negroes from the deep South. Both Negroes and Puerto Ricans are American citizens, but for these groups absorption into the urban life of America has been particularly painful. Today these groups, who are relatively new to the city, occupy the ghettos of the former immigrants. Today, among the problems common to nearly every city of any size is how to make the city a place in which these most recent newcomers can find the kind of comfort, glamor, and opportunity as did those who came before.

Why Are People Leaving the City?

You have already read that one aspect of the process of urbanization is the flight of those who can afford it from the central city. You have noted that, although people are leaving the city for the

Negroes were not absorbed into the urban job market as quickly as foreign immigrants. These latest migrants to our cities occupy the ghettoes of the former immigrants; however, the buildings are now sixty years older. (Jack Eisenberg-OEO)

suburbs, they must nevertheless properly be regarded as part of the urban area. But why do they leave? Where do they go? Are they satisfied when they get there?

The city dweller leaves the central city for the suburbs for many reasons. These reasons obviously differ from individual to individual and from family to family. However, the reasons why they leave grow out of many causes, not just one. The city dweller, for example, may begin his day by breathing in foul air and drinking impure water. The crush and crowd of the subway bring him to work ill prepared for the day ahead. He grabs his lunch from a crowded counter or cafeteria and returns to his home only after braving the subway rush hour once again. During the day he has been rubbing elbows with crowds; yet he is essentially alone. He does business with subordinates, superiors, competitors, and colleagues; yet he has few, if any, friends among them.

If he sends his children to a public school, they are probably not receiving a full day's schooling because of overcrowded conditions. The textbooks his children use are probably old and worn, as is the school building itself. If he lives in an apartment, he knows few if any of his neighbors. If he lives in a private house, his neighbors may be a bit farther away, but they are still too close to provide the family with a sense of spaciousness. If he has a car, it may be used mostly by his wife, if she can hazard the congestion of traffic snarls common to the central city.

In the meantime, the cost of living is high and appears to be mounting. Taxes have been increasing rapidly. The services the city has provided in the form of police and fire protection, sanitation, and opportunities for recreation seem hopelessly inadequate. While the city may be the center for cultural opportunities, including the theater and the opera, it takes such a great effort to return to the heart of the city during the evening in order to enjoy them that it often seems wiser to pass them up.

In addition, neighborhoods change. The slums seem to grow and crime seems to mount. Subways, parks, and playgrounds are unsafe or appear to be so, and the city dweller stays away, if he can, since he does not wish to take chances or expose his wife and children to possible danger. He begins to feel

The movement from the cities to the suburbs started in the 1950's, went on during the '60's, and will continue in the '70's. (John Huehnergarth)

A summer program called Pride, Inc., is a first step in cleaning up our cities. City services are so strained that they cannot possibly meet their needs without federal help. (Wide World)

One of the great advantages of the city is its many fine restaurants. (Milton Charles)

uneasy about his neighbors, as their skin color and spoken tongue may be different from his own. He may forget that he too was an immigrant or that he is only a generation or two removed from the struggles of his own family for the comforts and opportunities of the city. Although he may not wish to admit it, even to himself, hidden prejudice, of which he may not have been previously aware, rises to the surface. And he seeks to run away. He runs to the suburb.

Whether it be Shaker Heights in Cleveland or Highland Park in the Chicago area or Great Neck on Long Island, the suburb seems attractive. From the suburb he feels he can get to work in the central city in about the same amount of time it took him before, and in far greater comfort. It may cost somewhat more, but then again, while he may not be rich, he is prosperous enough to make the move and assume the additional cost. Only the very rich and the very poor seem to remain behind, although they obviously do so for different reasons. The homes in the suburbs have more room. The grounds encourage the cultivation of a lawn and a flower garden. Neighbors seem friendly and the schools are new. Opportunities for recreation exist and they seem to be easily accessible. Taxes, at least initially, seem lower; while the cost of living may not be much lower, if at all, there are many shops nearby to make shopping not only easy but a social event as well. The shopping areas have huge parking lots and the stores seem well stocked. Surely in the suburbs one can have the best of both possible worlds of urban living.

Has the Movement to the Suburbs Helped or Hurt the Central City?

When the movement to the suburbs began in the 1920s and speeded up after World War II, there was fear that the central city would die. This did not happen, nor is it likely to happen. The central city has remained the financial and business center of the metropolitan region. It remains the center of high finance and of high fashion and of a highly stimulating intellectual life. Yet the movement of people to the suburbs has harmed the city in many ways.

For one thing, the city became a place where mainly the rich and poor lived. The rich could insulate themselves from the poor in expensive town houses, luxurious apartments, and chauffeur-

Although you mostly hear about the poverty in the cities, it is a fact that some of the world's richest people also live there. (Joe Molnar)

driven cars and private schools. While they paid high taxes, their taxes were not enough to pay for the services the people needed. As the middle class left, property values fell, and the tax base further declined as industry in many cases began to find that it could function at least as efficiently and perhaps less expensively outside the city as inside it.

While taxable business property was decreasing, the services the poor required were multiplying. Housing deteriorated rapidly into slums and could not be replaced, repaired, or rebuilt speedily. The poor were largely Negro and Puerto Rican in-migrants who came to the city with less education, fewer skills, and fewer resources of their own for building a good life. The city tried to meet the needs of these groups in the way it had earlier tried to meet the needs of foreign immigrant groups. This attempt was, however, largely unsuccessful. The schools that had served the immigrant largely failed to serve the Negro adequately. Classes were too large, teachers were unavailable or inadequately prepared, methods of instruction were outworn, and the schools seemed unresponsive to the needs of the newcomer to the city.

The costs of welfare to help the poor mounted and relief rolls swelled. An inadequate police force found it increasingly difficult to curb crime and prevent delinquency. The tensions of the big city and the disappointment of Negroes and Puerto Ricans at not finding the promised opportunity burst into race riots. During the summer of 1967, Newark, Detroit, Cleveland, Milwaukee were the scenes of such riots. The riots demonstrated the great gap between the rich and the poor. They also dramatized the fact that the central city was not meeting its responsibilities adequately. And, making matters worse, the riots probably hastened the departure of more middle-class people to the suburbs, thus further reducing the possible wealth that could be taxed to provide the services now required.

Did the Middle Class Find What They Wanted in the Suburb?

The answer to this question is both yes and no. The middle class did find larger homes, spacious lawns, and neighbors more like themselves. But life in suburbia was not really all it was made out to be. For one thing, as more and more people moved to the outskirts of the city, traffic congestion followed. The trip to work became as much of an ordeal as it had ever been on the subway; roads that once were

One problem in the city schools is that predominantly white, middle-class teachers are finding it harder to communicate with the growing numbers of nonwhite, lower-class students. (Joe Molnar)

adequate to meet the needs of the suburbanite soon proved hopelessly behind the times. Because the suburb was largely a bedroom community, it lacked a tax base to support the building of schools and the provision of other community services. At first, new suburbanites were willing to help by paying high property taxes on their homes. They felt that in this way their children could have "the best." But, in time, taxes became prohibitively high, even for this group. There were few large industries that could be relied on to share the tax burden. As a result, the services the city dweller hoped to find in suburbia began to diminish. In suburbia, too, schools became overcrowded, traffic congestion mounted, police and fire protection and sanitation collection were not all that had originally been hoped for.

The life style in suburbia tended to be dull and monotonous. During the day it was a community of women and children. Privacy, of which there had perhaps been too much in the city, was almost unknown. Women got together in car pools to drive their children to and from school, religious services and instructions, and the country clubs of which they had become members. When the men returned at night there was no place to go other than to visit a neighbor or attend a PTA meeting. Since all suburbanites were in similar financial circumstances, keeping up with the Joneses became a serious occupation. If one's neighbor made the cellar into a playroom, one had to follow suit or be left behind. If my neighbor had two cars, why not me?

As their children grew up and the need for big houses and better schools diminished, some of the suburbanites have returned to the central city. Indeed, there is reason to believe that the central city may be gaining a new lease on life; its advantages are better understood and appreciated, while its shortcomings are being more vigorously attacked. Actually, city and suburb, both part of the process of urbanization, must work together if the people in both are to prosper. Neither city nor suburb can fail to take the other into account. It is because they have failed to do so for so long that such hard problems have developed for each. The future of metropolitan areas depends on finding a better way of harnessing the resources of city and suburb and planning for the years ahead.

This scene of the Los Angeles Freeway shows that commuting has become a way of life for the suburbanite. (American Airlines)

How May Cities Be More Effectively Planned?

Many of the ills associated with city and suburban life are the result of lack of planning. The effects on the city of the streetcar, the subway, the automobile were essentially not anticipated. Instead, new patterns of growth were thrust upon older existing structures. It is this lack of planning that has led to

57

People living in the city often weigh the shortcomings against the advantages. There is no perfect place to live, and many people still prefer the city. (Drawing by James Flora)

What provisions should long-range planning make

Probs

traffic jams, slums, congestion, air and water pollution, and mounting crime. By "planning" we mean taking into account those forces that are shaping the city and looking ahead in order to change them if necessary or provide for them if possible. In most modern cities, such "looking ahead" has not been effectively done. Yet this lack of adequate provision for the future is strange, since America's history shows a strong concern for city planning.

As early as 1638, New Haven, Connecticut, had a plan for its growth. Indeed, Yale University is located where it is partly because of this plan. And, in its day, it was regarded as a model, which was worth following and which would provide for the future needs and growth of the city. In 1682, William Penn laid out a plan for the projected growth of Philadelphia, using the "gridiron" design of straight streets with side streets crossing them at right angles. Penn's scheme allowed for ample open areas and for a pattern of houses that would give the residents of Philadelphia the advantages of living

living space

*why imp.   psych.   pattern
refreshing*

New cities and parts of cities are being planned, but whether they will finally be accepted and built depends on money, politicking, and other factors. This is a plan of Battery Park City in lower Manhattan, being designed by the architectural firms of Harrison and Abromovitz, Philip Johnson, and Conklin and Rossant. (Louis Checkman)

closely together without the disadvantages of crowding. Much of the layout of Manhattan, in 1811, was based on the plan of William Penn. And after the American Revolution, in 1791, a Frenchman, Pierre Charles L'Enfant, had been hired to plan the nation's capital in Washington, D.C. L'Enfant used a rectangular pattern in which the Capitol was the center and all streets radiated from it, with cross streets encircling the radii. These plans, while often bold and imaginative, were never fully realized. For

59

This sketch of Philadelphia in 1800 shows one of the oldest cities planned and built in the United States. (New York Public Library Picture Collection)

the most part, cities outgrew their original boundaries, and the plans did not make allowance for the changing needs of the cities.

Today, city planning has become an art as well as a science. It involves, for example, the setting aside of some areas for housing and others for industry. It involves zoning to make the best use of the land, so that what is built will not be entirely the result of the blind pursuit of profit. Suburban areas have been almost as guilty as the central city of a failure to plan. Thus, shopping centers are often built too close to residential communities, and bars and poolrooms begin to be found in these neighborhoods. Building standards have not been observed, so that shoddy housing, even in the suburbs, exists side by side with more durable structures. Failure to plan adequately for storms and for sewage has meant flooding of highways and basements.

Today planning must take many forms. It involves

the urban renewal of older neighborhoods. It must be regional in nature to take into account the inter-relations that exist between city and suburb. Provision must be made not only for housing, but for adequate industry; the plan must provide for job-creating industries on the one hand and adequate schools on the other, not only to provide effective workers and professionals, but to make the good life possible.

While planning can anticipate many of the problems that cities face, cities have been slow to act. Probably the greatest obstacle to effective planning has been the many governments of which the metropolitan regions are composed. Fear of higher taxes, fear of loss of power, fear that special interests and privileges may be lost have prevented these governments from working together. The federal government is beginning to help in many ways. Yet unless local governments "hang together," they may all "hang separately," as slums, vice, crime, poverty destroy the city and suburb as good places in which to live.

What Is the Future of the City?

No one is wise enough to be able to say for certain what the future of the city will really be. Surely the city will be far different from what it is today. It probably will be more spread out than ever before, although it is equally likely that a central hub, which will be the commercial heart of the city, will still be identifiable. New modes of transportation, and other technological changes will alter the appearance of the city and change the relationships that exist among cities and between the central city and the suburb.

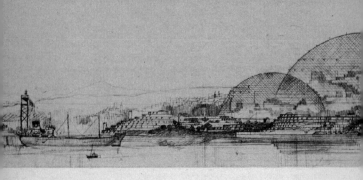

New political forms will probably have to develop so that city and suburb can work together with the state and federal government in planning for future growth. As part of such planning one can look forward to the development of so-called "New Towns," which are self-contained communities in which, it is hoped, the good life can be enjoyed by all. In such towns an effort is made to obtain a balance between home and industry. This is done not only to provide jobs but also to provide tax support for the services the community needs. Reston, Virginia, which was started with public funds and has recently begun to be supported by funds from private industry, is one example of a New Town. New Towns provide for variety in housing accommodations— large apartment houses, garden apartments, row houses, and detached private homes.

Usually there is provision for a well-located shopping center, and ample space is given to greenways, grass-covered areas that connect the various parts of the New Town. Such communities are usually limited in size, but what the best size should be is not always clear. What is clear is that in these New Towns there seems to be provision made for variety

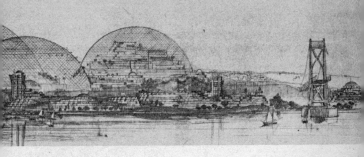

Poughkeepsie rejected these plans for a domed city. Many progressive plans for cities never get accepted because the local governments consider them too extreme. (Conklin and Rossant, architects)

and growth, but not so much growth as to promote the congestion and indifference commonly associated with large cities. The best size for a city has been a problem that has been debated since Plato and Aristotle in ancient Greece gave their attention to it. It is still a problem which has not been settled, nor will it be settled soon.

"The future potential for the urban complex is great. Our tools for achieving this potential are imperfect and are still in the process of development. But a nation which is affluent, which is willing to face up to social problems and which is excited by its possibilities has a real future."[17]

But whether or not the future will be as bright as it can be is open to question. The biggest question is: Will public and private interests make possible adequate city planning, or will self-interest, greed, and desire for immediate gain continue to lead to hasty gratification and leisurely repentance? Will the city meet the challenge posed by the current wave

The Bryan Woods neighborhood center is in Columbia, Maryland, one of the "New Towns." Every neighborhood center will consist of a swimming pool, a convenience store, a child day-care center, and an elementary school. (Robert C. Lautman—The Rouse Company, architects)

of newcomers it must now serve? And will the newcomers follow the example of the older settlers and also move to the suburbs?

One theory of American history holds that America became great because of the existence of a frontier. On the frontier, initiative, independence, self-reliance were encouraged. Democracy was made possible, since a man was judged on what he could do, not who he was. The frontier of today is urban, not rural.[18] To the virtues that made conquering the

In another "New Town," Reston, Virginia, the townhouses
were built above the stores in the central shopping area.
(Conklin and Rossant, architects)

wilderness possible must be added others, which have always been at work but have not been sufficiently appreciated. These virtues are cooperation and a willingness to share in making the city all that it is capable of being.

Part Two

Selected Readings

What constitutes a city—number of people, size, density of population, function—is the subject of this article. Is it possible to arrive at a standard definition of a city acceptable to all countries?

1

What Is a Town?

by EMRYS JONES

EVERY country has to have a definition of towns and cities for census purposes, and a glance at some of these will illustrate the variety of definitions. Some countries adopt a simple numerical

From Emrys Jones, *Towns and Cities* (London: Oxford University Press [paperback], 1966), pp. 3–4. Reprinted by permission.

value. A town or city is bigger than a village community, and if we are dealing with very large settlements there is often little doubt. But at the lower end of the scale, if size is the criterion, who is to say what the size of a town is? In Denmark a settlement of 200 people constitutes a town, as it does in Sweden and Finland. In Greece a settlement must have over 10,000 inhabitants before it can be called a town. Between these is a great variety of figures. A thousand inhabitants makes a town in Canada, but 2,500 in the United States. A thousand is enough in Venezuela, but there must be 5,000 people to make a town in Ghana. Clearly numbers alone mean very little. There are circumstances in which a numerically small settlement may have urban characteristics . . . others in which a numerically large settlement may be . . . a village in which the vast majority of men are farmers. The latter is certainly the case in agricultural states and in the developing countries. In India, for example, it is specified that to be a town a settlement must not only have more than 5,000 inhabitants, but its density must be over 1,000 to a square mile, and over 75% of its adult male population must be engaged in work other than agriculture.

This last definition suggests other criteria, namely density and function. We certainly think of most cities as being densely populated, though this need not be universally true. But with the exception of India, density is rarely used as a criterion. More critical than density is function, for it is generally accepted that one of the distinguishing characteristics of a town or city is the fact that its work is

The Spanish Steps in Rome provide a place where people can rest and enjoy a leisurely hour. (Italian Government Travel Office)

divorced from the soil: its people are not primarily food-producers. Yet very few states include function in the definition, partly because it is implied in most as an urban characteristic. India, as we have seen, defines this function accurately. Israel refuses the status of a town to settlements of over 2,000 if more than a third of the heads of households are engaged in agriculture; and the Congo accepts the figure of 2,000 with the proviso that they must be predominantly non-agricultural.

The administrative function of a town is most clearly brought out by those states who use this as a sole criterion. This is so in Turkey, Czechoslovakia, the Dominican Republic, and the United Arab Republic. Many more define their towns by giving them a certain kind of government, as in Algeria, Japan, Tunisia, and, most familiar, the United Kingdom. This really means that the city or town is so by definition—a town is what the state is prepared to call a town. This does not help us very much. It is even more frustrating when a solecism is introduced as in Rumania, where a town is a settlement having urban characteristics. The wheel has come full circle. As one writer put it despairingly, "A city is a city is a city."

While cities have often been pictured as crime-ridden, unhealthy places to live, the country life has been praised as wholesome and "ideal." In this selection the author weighs the evidence and gives a balanced account of the country, the suburb, and the city.

2

Country, Suburb, City

by DOROTHY BARCLAY

ARE cities unhealthy? At one time they certainly were. The great plagues of history flourished in cities. In this country until comparatively recently, diseases such as smallpox, diphtheria, typhoid fever took a tremendous toll every year among city dwellers. Sixty years or so ago a New Yorker could expect to live a shorter life by seven years than the

From Dorothy Barclay, *Understanding the City Child: A Book for Parents* (New York: Franklin Watts, 1959), pp. 7–9. Reprinted by permission of the publisher.

average elsewhere in the nation where comparable records were kept. Today whatever difference exists is so small as to be negligible. Opportunities for good health and long life are now at least as good in the city as in the country, with some statistics even favoring the city dwellers.

Are cities destructive of mental health? Mental health is a factor far harder to measure than physical survival—but researchers are trying. All kinds of complications of definition, measurement, and comparison arise. However, two painstaking studies —one made in an isolated part of eastern Canada, the other in the heart of a congested American city—revealed a thought-provoking point: the same proportion of mentally healthy and mentally ill people was found in the big city as in the small town.

Are cities crime-ridden, rural areas pure? Uniform crime reports of the F.B.I. indicate crime on the increase in both city and country, with rural crime in recent years increasing more rapidly. Comparative figures can be misleading, to be sure, but any clear-eyed observer can notice what many of the world's best writers have made plain—that rural life is by no means the innocent existence that city dwellers sometimes dream it to be. As David Riesman has pointed out, the pieties that do exist in small-town life are often possible only because of the "export of adventure" to the cities. Such pieties, what's more, he added, are likely to be exaggerated in the minds of city people "unfamiliar with the forms rural deviance takes."

There are several oases within the city where you can sit and relax. (The Museum of Modern Art, New York)

Is country living "ideal" for children? Not if the criticisms of rural observers are to be fully credited. Isolation, meager educational opportunities, and lack of intellectual stimulation are characteristics of the true rural life—not to be confused with the type of "country" life often made possible for basically "city" people by virtue of city-earned incomes, background, and experience.

Is suburban living, then, the perfect answer? There are all kinds of suburbs, all kinds of city neighborhoods, and all kinds of families. No respectable researcher would attempt to give a firm answer to this question. However, one deep and searching study . . . has revealed that with all the love, attention, and "advantages" that well-to-do parents and devoted teachers could provide, the youngsters of the suburban community studied (judged on the basis of standardized tests) had no better mental health—and perhaps worse—than children from less "ideal" surroundings. In fact, the suburban boys and girls claimed many times the number of physical complaints and symptoms claimed by a group of city youngsters of the same age. On tests designed to measure such delicate matters as "sense of personal freedom," "feeling of belonging," "sense of personal worth," social standards, social skills, and family relations, the children of this privileged suburb rated from slightly to significantly worse than the mixed group of children elsewhere on whom the test was standardized.

The drawbacks of life for adults in the new suburbia have been widely aired in recent years: the added strain on fathers of time spent in commuting, the resultant lack of time for the children; the special chores and burdens of maintaining a house and grounds without paid help, the over-organiza-

Exhibitions like this one of works by Giacometti allow busy city people to enjoy a pleasant workday break. (The Museum of Modern Art, New York)

tion of life; the pressure to conform to others in appearance, possessions, activities, even attitudes and ideas; the social competitiveness of some communities, often complicated by a feeling of exposure to others' criticisms.

None of this is meant to suggest that country living or suburban living is bad for children. It is reported merely to underscore the fact that city living is not necessarily bad for children either. The community in which a child grows up will have its influence on his development. The most important influence, however, wherever he lives, will be his family. But the community in which they live affects family life too.

The city lured immigrants from Europe
as it did migrants from rural America.
This selection shows how and why they
settled in the cities.

3

The Lure of the City

by BLAKE MCKELVEY

THE study of urban census data received greater
attention as the period drew to a close, but
no statistical analysis could depict the rich com-
plexity of the human elements that peopled the

1915 (New Brunswick, N.J.: Rutgers University Press, 1963),
pp. 65–67. Copyright © 1963 by Rutgers, the State University.
Reprinted by permission of the publisher.

American city. As the decades advanced, the immigrant tide became increasingly diversified. By 1880 Germans had displaced the Irish as the dominant minority in most of the great cities, and these two groups continued for another decade to hold first or second place in all but Boston and Detroit, where Canadians, taking second place, outnumbered the Germans and the Irish respectively, and at Minneapolis where Canadians took second place to the Swedes, with Norwegians a close third. This was only the beginning, for the next decade saw eastern and southern Europeans crowding the poorer districts of all major cities. By 1900 the Poles had become the second largest minority in Buffalo and Milwaukee; the Austrians held that position in Cleveland, the Russians in Baltimore, the Italians in New Orleans, and the British in Los Angeles.

The increased representation of these later arrivals became more striking after the turn of the century. Many of their predecessors were achieving positions of influence not only in such centers of concentration as St. Louis, Chicago, and Milwaukee, but in a host of other places. In San Francisco the wide diversity from the start deprived any one group of a leading role and gave the community a cosmopolitan character. In Minneapolis, on the other hand, the Scandinavians were sufficiently numerous to overshadow other immigrant groups; they played an active role in the city and made it, in effect, the Scandinavian capital of America, the center of Swedish and Norwegian papers, churches, and seminaries.

In most cases, however, the immigrants, who generally arrived after the city's development was well launched, crowded into the poorer districts,

Immigrants to the United States came from Asia as well as Europe. Orientals were excluded and their entry restricted as early as the 1880's. (Jacob A. Riss Collection—Museum of the City of New York)

where lodging was cheap, or built sprawling settlements on the outskirts. These ethnic colonies,
whether large or small, served as magnets for late
comers from each land. There the weary migrant
could find friends able and willing to listen to his
story and to help him find a job and a home. An
element of chance had no doubt brought the first
small groups of Poles to Buffalo, Milwaukee, and
Chicago in the seventies, but within a decade these
attracted thousands of their fellow countrymen, who
hastily established numerous institutions and erected
congenial, if crowded, homes often in their native
style. By the end of the period Chicago's Polish
district ranked next to Warsaw and Lodz in size.
Several other foreign neighborhoods in the great
metropolitan centers achieved a similar distinction,
which encouraged the establishment of old-country
churches and other institutions and fostered a nostalgic revival of native handicrafts and customs.

The Russian Jews and Italians, who took first
and second place from the Germans and the Irish
in New York City after 1900, also crowded the
work benches and labor gangs of many other places.
Newly industrialized towns of modest size—some of
which, like Burlington, Vermont, had escaped earlier
migrations—now attracted a fresh influx from
abroad. The challenge these newcomers presented
to old customs often proved startling in such communities, but most northern cities had long since become familiarly patched by nationality settlements.
Foreign travelers who wandered off Main Street had
frequently to remind themselves that this was America and not some European country.

A ghetto area on New York's Lower East Side, c. 1900.
(History Division, Los Angeles County Museum of Natural
History)

Urban problems have been part of the American dilemma for over a hundred years. Although the situation looks more critical today, this author believes that it only seems more serious because of the increased attention of the communications media and the public. In fact, he says that things are better in our cities today than they were sixty years ago. Do you agree with this point of view?

4

The Urban Problem

by RAYMOND VERNON

A NYONE who has had the opportunity to review the history of American cities cannot fail to be struck with the fact that the things we speak of as urban problems have been with us in some form for a very long time. If transportation is a part of the problem, as it surely is in anyone's analysis, we find evidence that the problem was acute for a considerable group of urban dwellers as far back as the early nineteenth century. Before the Civil War, New

From Raymond Vernon, *The Myth and Reality of Our Urban Problems* (Cambridge, Mass.: Harvard University Press, 1966), pp. 3–11. Copyright © 1962, 1966 by the President and Fellows of Harvard College. Reprinted by permission of the publishers.

York's downtown streets were already a jumble of brewery drays, horse trolleys, hackney coaches, and steam locomotives; so desperate was New York's citizenry over the situation that it even built overhead crosswalks to bridge the equestrian battle field of lower Broadway. By 1900, according to contemporary photographs, the scramble of traffic was endemic in extensive downtown areas of our eastern cities. By 1925, the automobile was already creating intolerable waiting conditions at the major river crossings in and near the big cities of the East, as ferryboats struggled valiantly with the rising tide of traffic. By 1930, the mass transit facilities of practically all the major cities were filled to bursting in rush hours, reaching peaks of discomfort for the middle- and low-income commuter which have probably never since been matched.

If housing is an aspect of the urban problem, then the urban problem again must be thought of as very old. In the mid-nineteenth century, every major city of the United States embraced teeming slums whose conditions of life were so incredibly shocking —shocking even by the middle-class standards of the time—as to make the contemporary slum areas of East St. Louis and South Philadelphia appear benign by contrast. When Mrs. O'Leary's cow wiped out half of Chicago in 1871, she forced the re-

This is a picture of Longacre Square (now Times Square) in 1900. These horse-drawn carriages were later replaced by the automobile and the city trains (Museum of the City of New York)

building of a city which had largely been a collection of poor shacks and hovels. When San Francisco's great fire of 1906 destroyed much of her Chinatown, it wiped out a teeming slum of indescribable squalor. The evidence provided by the prints of the nineteenth century tells us also that, in addition to containing large slums at their ancient cores, the large cities of the United States typically were surrounded by ex-

tensive shanty-towns consisting of shelters that were only a cut or two above a frontier lean-to.

If crime and delinquency are measures of the urban problem, the impressionistic evidence suggests that in long-run secular terms the problem may actually have declined substantially. Most major cities of the nineteenth and early twentieth century contained areas in which law and order simply were not applied and in which anarchy or gang rule was

THE FUNERAL OF OLD TAMMANY.

The nineteenth-century political bosses were so firmly entrenched in the cities that cartoonists had a hard time arousing public opinion against them. (Museum of the City of New York)

allowed to go unchallenged. Instead of having neighborhoods in which patrolmen plied their beats in pairs, many cities had neighborhoods which never saw the authority of law in any form. Chinese tongs were the law for many of San Francisco's impoverished inhabitants, while warring gangs were the recognized authority for many of New York's immigrant Irish and Italians.

If the quality of public service constitutes a measure of our urban difficulties, then there is no doubt that the secular trend has been one of improvement rather than decline. The history of American cities throughout the nineteenth century is punctuated with accounts of epidemics generated by polluted water supplies, of streets rendered impassable by mud and water, of great fires allowed to rage unchecked because of the pitiful inadequacy of fire fighting equipment, and of corrupted and compliant courts and police.

Reliable water and sewage services, dependable fire fighting facilities, streetcleaning and snow removal brigades, efforts to deal with air and water pollution, are much more a product of the twentieth than of the nineteenth century in most American cities.

Yet no one will deny that discontent with our urban setting is being articulated more forcefully than at any time in our recent history. In this sense, we have an "urban problem."

Megalopolis was the site of an ancient Greek city which was to have
become the greatest in the world. It
failed, but the name has lived on, and
today it refers to the northeastern section of the country extending from
Boston to Washington, D.C.

5

Main Street
of the Nation

by WOLF VON ECKARDT

FOR the nation as a whole, Megalopolis is what
Main Street is for most communities.

It is the place where government, most of the
banks, the big offices, the newspapers and broadcasting stations, the important stores, the schools, libraries and theaters are concentrated.

From Wolf Von Eckardt, *The Challenge of Megalopolis: A
Twentieth Century Fund Report* (New York: The Macmillan Com-
pany, 1964), pp. 11–13. Reprinted by permission of The Twentieth
Century Fund, Inc.

It is the place where policies, decisions and fashions, or most of them, are made for the entire community. If Main Street is booming, the whole community prospers.

The same is true of Megalopolis in respect to the nation. It can be said, in fact, that the economic, political and cultural life of Megalopolis has become an essential factor in the economic, political and cultural life of the entire free world.

Foreign visitors rarely see more of America than Megalopolis, just as passing visitors in a town rarely see more than a few blocks of Main Street.

The pre-eminence of Megalopolis is rooted in history. The region is first in power and influence largely because it was here that the United States of America first began to emerge. The Pilgrims landed here. It was on the northeastern seaboard that the colonies declared their independence and the nation was born. And here, for three centuries, was the gateway for the transcontinental march of settlement.

As a result of that march, ours is now a highly developed continent. It boasts at least two other concentrations of urban clusters, riches, economic equipment and educated people—the industrialized Midwest, between the Great Lakes and the Ohio River, and the California seaboard. But Megalopolis shows no signs of relinquishing its pre-eminent position to these. On the contrary, it continues to assume more of the Main Street functions than ever.

The impact of the Federal government in Washington on the everyday life of people throughout the country is not apt to lessen, regardless of politics. As the technological age becomes more complex, people are forced to specialize in their pursuits to earn their living. The more we specialize, the more

Downtown New York is the financial capital of the world. In this section of the city, two 110-story government buildings are being built, as well as a possible new city complex. (American Airlines)

need we have for central coordination of our common efforts in all our public activities.

When Washington was planned and built just below the falls of the Potomac, its planners expected it to develop into a great seaport and commercial center. Instead, it remained specialized as a city which serves the Federal government almost exclusively. And, as the nation grew, it also became an international center. This does not mean, however, that political and economic policy making are, or ever have been, divorced. This would be impossible. Washington simply did not need to develop into an industrial and economic center because such centers are nearby and also within Megalopolis.

The nation's money market is, of course, predominantly located in New York. The largest financial institutions and the nation's two important security exchanges are in downtown Manhattan. And New York shares its tremendous concentration of financial power only with other Megalopolitan centers, mainly Boston, Philadelphia and, lately, Washington. Through the Securities and Exchange Commission and the Federal Reserve Board, Washington exercises the necessary controls over the money market. Since Federal expenditures and the trading in U.S. government securities are becoming increasingly important, Washington also plays a substantial part in the world of finance.

The insurance industry, too, which started in Megalopolis, is still mainly concentrated there.

Finance and management have become inseparable just as have political and economic policies. All managerial decision-making for industry and commerce, in fact, is deeply interwoven with financial problems. That is why most of the country's large corporations, no matter where their production centers may be, keep adding their imposing headquarters palaces to the skylines of Megalopolis.

Mass communications are almost exclusively concentrated in Megalopolis. One of the most important raw materials of the office industry is information. The counting houses of old have grown into huge banks, stock exchanges and insurance companies. The exchanges of news and gossip on the street and in taverns has been replaced by the great newspapers, the magazines, the broadcasting corporations and advertising.

And as we all know, Times Square and Madison Avenue wield the same influence on the nation's mass communications media as Wall Street and the midtown banks wield on the nation's financial affairs.

We need not elaborate on the influence of the big radio and television corporations on local stations and listeners across the country. Broadcasting is licensed in Washington, and the networks—CBS, NBC and ABC—are all headquartered in New York. Broadcasting stations, like newspapers, are local, of course. But the vast majority of them are affiliated with the big networks.

Madison Avenue dominates advertising and while not all big advertising agencies have their offices on that street, just about all of the large and influential

Reading rooms, like this one in the New York Public Library, are a necessity for city dwellers. (Sam Faulk-Monkmeyer)

ones have their offices in Megalopolis. Again, this is quite logical, considering that both their clients (the industrial and commercial corporations) and their outlets (the mass communications media) are located there.

The complex modern integration of business and culture is demonstrated by the dependency of the mass communications media on advertising. Advertising accounts for 70 percent of the total revenue of newspapers, 60 percent of the revenue of magazines and 90 percent of the income of television stations.

Public relations, a relatively new and pervasive aspect of our culture, is also more prevalent in Megalopolis than elsewhere.

A thirst for education and culture developed early in our history. As soon as our new society was settled sufficiently to do so, it established colleges, universities, symphony orchestras, theaters and museums. Again the area between New Hampshire and Maryland had a head start in building reputation and nationwide influence.

Such names as Harvard, Yale and Princeton, the New York Philharmonic, the Metropolitan Museum of Art, the Philadelphia Art Museum and the Enoch Pratt Library in Baltimore speak for themselves.

The combined libraries of Megalopolis, for instance, contain some 100 million volumes. That is one third of the number in the whole United States.

Book publishing, too, is all but exclusively concentrated in Megalopolis. A few book publishers are located elsewhere, and college and university presses are scattered across the country. But editors, authors and book salesmen tend to gravitate towards New York.

This concentration of skills, learning and talent, which, of course, goes hand in hand with the concentration of educational and cultural institutions, also attracts the foundations which support so much of our research, education, culture and charity.

The key to this concentration is skilled and educated people. There are, as we have seen, few natural resources which would account for this snowballing of services and functions in one small part of the country. Nor does the historic head start account for all of it.

A more important factor is human organization. It is a fact that government, finance, corporation management and all manner of educational, research and cultural institutions require more or less highly trained and specialized employees.

The presence and activities of these people and their organizations, in turn, produce more trained and specialized personnel. And this, again, spawns more institutions and organizations or draws them to Megalopolis.

An often gaudy, often dismal ugliness pervades much of Megalopolis, as it does many an American Main Street. There are the beer cans on the highway, the billboards and the jazzy, Disneyland roadside stands and motels. In many of its cities the air is no longer clean. The noise is deafening. The water is polluted. Traffic and transportation are becoming a nightmare. Slums and "grey areas" continue to spread.

Yet, despite these much criticized facts, the crowded people of Megalopolis are extremely fortunate. They form, on the average, the richest, best-educated, best-housed, and best-serviced group of [any of] similar size in the world.

Sometimes a story can illustrate facts more persuasively than a documentary account. This fable emphasizes the ills of the nation's cities and suggests farsighted cures.

6

A Fable of American Cities

by WILFRED OWEN

THERE once was a nation of 200 million people that was the most powerful country in all the world. At the national level the inhabitants were very rich, but at the local level they often turned out to be quite poor. And, as luck would have it, they all lived at the local level.

Seventy per cent of the population was crowded into 1 per cent of the land, which they called cities. One fifth of the city people were the victims of poverty. Many of them lived in slums where housing was unfit for living, schools unfit for learning, and the air unfit for breathing. To top it off, the urbanites were always getting stuck in traffic.

Now the leaders of the people decided that what the urbanites needed most was expressways to get the rich through the blighted areas faster, and subways to keep the poor from seeing how bad things were on the surface.

But the cities continued to grow uglier and the frustrations greater, and, while the people were moving more, they were liking it less. And there were riots in the street.

Now the trouble with the urbanites was that they were always caught up with the problems because they were always caught up in the symptoms. Traffic congestion was one of them. The reason for traffic congestion was basically that too many people were crowding into too little space, and without the semblance of community plans. In addition the cities had old-fashioned streets never designed to move traffic, and lined on both sides with parked cars to make sure they didn't.

The urbanites left no open space to balance off the built up areas that generated traffic, and they put their housing as far as possible from the places people worked.

So the possibility of getting a job was often missed by the impossibility of getting anywhere near it.

The commuting problem was compounded by an ancient tribal custom. People with light complexions worked close in and lived way out, while people with dark complexions were expected to work way out and live close in. As a result, the urbanites were always trying to get from where they shouldn't be to where they shouldn't have to go, and they all tried to get there at the same time.

Now there were certain wise men in that country who saw that the so-called transportation problem was really part of the larger problem of urban design.

The basic trouble, said the wise men, is not how badly people move, but how bleakly they live. What we need is trees and grass and fresh air, decent houses and schools, and convenient recreation. People should spend their time enjoying the city instead of spending their money escaping it.

When the leaders of the country heard this, they decided to put one man in charge of cities full time, just as the nation had a man at the top to worry about fighting the enemy. This was a good idea, because the enemy turned out to be the cities, and the cities were a lot closer to home.

The chief urban worrier lost no time doing the things that cost the least and showed up the best.

The obvious first step was to clear the streets of vehicles that were parking, double parking, or cruising in the hope of parking. These vehicles were destroying whatever transportation capacity there was, and they were making neighborhoods look like assembly lines. Never had so much space been used to help so few at the expense of so many.

The answer was the Off-Street Parking and Playground Act, which made loans to finance attractive multi-level garages in cities agreeing to ban parking on the streets. Service stations were included within these structures to help pay the bill, and play space was provided on the roof.

The effect was to double street capacity, reduce congestion, improve safety, decrease noise, make room for curbside planting, and increase the livability of neighborhoods. Traffic was improved 25 percent and the scenery 100 percent.

This policeman demonstrates one way of eliminating cars parked in a crowded shopping area. For the customer it is an expensive and irritating experience. (Shalmon Bernstein)

The second step was to take the rush out of the rush hour.

The Staggered Hours Act offered tax concessions to all companies willing to schedule worker arrivals after 9 o'clock. The size of the tax rebate increased for each quarter hour beyond 9 o'clock. Cities were able to compensate for the reduction in taxes by the reduction in congestions and, therefore, the lower cost of providing the necessary highways, and public transit.

The rush hour was further tamed by charging

Recreation in the city, like anywhere else, means having fun with your friends. (Joe Molnar)

half price for a transit ride or a parking space after 10 o'clock.

Employers and workers had long resisted staggering work hours on the grounds that this would decrease productivity, disturb sleeping habits, destroy

car pools, and disrupt dinner, and undermine the family. But all it did was reduce congestion.

The next step was to close the gap between home and work by letting people of all colors live where they wanted to. This restored the nation's image as well as the function of the central city. For now the center could provide the cultural and entertainment focus and the specialized activities for all the people of the metropolis.

The next legislation was the Transit Riders Protection Act of 1966, designed to pay homage to those brave people of the nation who rode in public conveyances. Street networks were designed for buses only, and buses were built that were quiet and sweet smelling and that people could get into.

It was stipulated that riders should be told where the bus was going, and when the next stop was coming. Metropolitan-area transit was scheduled by computer, and the whole works displayed electronically at each stop.

The revenues of all transport media were pooled to pay the bill for regional transportation systems by road and rail and in the air.

But the emancipation of transit riders caused ferment among pedestrians, who were the lowest caste of all the urbanites. Under the banner "Walkers of the World Unite!" they vowed to get the city back on its feet by getting the people back on theirs. "If we can walk in space," they said, "why can't we have space to walk in?" They built shopping plazas and campus-type neighborhoods, they air-conditioned the sidewalks, and they introduced benches, protective covering, and geraniums. Small electric cars were made available on the pedestrian mall for people who liked the idea of walking but refused to become involved.

The next step was sheer genius. Since much of the money available to improve the cities was earmarked for highways, highways were located where they would clear out slums and blight, and they were used to protect and insulate neighborhoods and industrial parks.

Elevated highways were banned. For the people knew that when highways were elevated, neighborhoods were depressed, but when highways were depressed, neighborhoods were elevated.

In the interests of fair play, the next step was to make urban renewal money available to help build highways.

This money was a supplementary fund to pay the additional costs of better landscaping, of building roadside parks, and of locating the highways where they cost more but looked better. So, in the end, transportation contributed to urban renewal, and urban renewal contributed to better transportation. The Bureau of the Budget was ecstatic. Instead of costing too much, the whole program cost nothing. For, in the end, the value of redesigned cities was many times the value of the slums, and human values had been multiplied by a more noble environment and by millions of jobs in urban reconstruction.

But it came to pass that while the old cities were being rebuilt, the urban population continued to grow and sprawl, and slums were being transported to the suburbs. The whole countryside was becoming a shambles of billboards, banners, beer parlors and barbecued beefburgers.

Another 100 million city dwellers would in one generation demand more new accommodations than had been built in all the nation's history.

Then the top man in charge of cities began to look around at the 99 percent of the country that was hardly being used.

There were places where the climate was cool,

the mountains high and the recreation opportunities good in both winter and summer; and there were places that had industrial potentials, research capabilities, resources, endowments and not too many people. And, in an age of air transport and satellite communications, these places that were once peripheral were now practically convenient.

So the people selected a thousand locations where new cities should be built or existing small towns enlarged. It was the purpose of this "national plan for cities" not only to preserve sites for urban settlement, but to preserve surrounding areas in forest and farm, and in State and National parks. Then joint public-private corporations designed and built the planned communities that were pleasant to live in and easy to move around in.

When the urbanites saw the sparkling new towns and the beauty of the restored cities, they could hardly believe their eyes. Now they saw it was possible to be urbanized and civilized as well as motorized and mechanized. For they had learned four basic rules for solving the problems of urbanization:

1. The principal problem of cities is not how to move, but how to live.

2. Improving the conditions of living can do more than anything else to reduce the need for moving.

3. But providing transportation is not just a matter of getting things moved. It is also a major means of improving the urban environment.

4. Looked at in this way, transportation has ceased to be a problem, because technology and systems techniques have made it a solution.

One of the most popular forms of entertainment in the city is the outdoor theater, like the Paper Bag Players who perform for the children of New York City. (Joe Molnar)

Then the urbanites burst into laughter to think how stupid they had been, and they thanked all the people in public and private life whose efforts had made the urban revolution possible. And they called themselves the Grateful Society.

But there were some urbanites who refused to laugh or even to be grateful, and they stood around in small groups shaking their heads and wondering. If our country is so rich, they said, why were the cities so poor? And, to this day, no one has been able to answer that question.

A noted critic of American cities, Jane Jacobs, describes how a neighborhood can become a healthful and happy place for man to live in. Even when a neighborhood appears to be physically run-down, it may yet have a character that makes effective living possible.

7

The Uses of City Neighborhoods

by JANE JACOBS

NEIGHBORHOOD is a word that has come to sound like a Valentine. As a sentimental concept, "neighborhood" is harmful to city planning. It leads to attempts at warping city life into imitations of town or suburban life. Sentimentality plays with sweet intentions in place of good sense.

From Jane Jacobs, *The Death and Life of Great American Cities* (New York: Random House, 1961), pp. 112–117 and 139–140. Copyright © 1961 by Jane Jacobs. Reprinted by permission of Random House, Inc.

A successful city neighborhood is a place that keeps sufficiently abreast of its problems so it is not destroyed by them. An unsuccessful neighborhood is a place that is overwhelmed by its defects and problems and is progressively more helpless before them. Our cities contain all degrees of success and failure. But on the whole we Americans are poor at handling city neighborhoods, as can be seen by the long accumulations of failures in our great gray belts on the one hand, and by the Turfs of rebuilt city on the other hand.

It is fashionable to suppose that certain touchstones of the good life will create good neighborhoods—schools, parks, clean housing and the like. How easy life would be if this were so! How charming to control a complicated and ornery society by bestowing upon it rather simple physical goodies. In real life, cause and effect are not so simple. Thus a Pittsburgh study, undertaken to show the supposed clear correlation between better housing and improved social conditions, compared delinquency records in still uncleared slums to delinquency records in new housing projects, and came to the embarrassing discovery that the delinquency was higher in the improved housing. Does this mean improved shelter increases delinquency? Not at all. It means other things may be more important than housing, however, and it means also that there is no direct, simple relationship between good housing and good behavior, a fact which the whole tale of the Western world's history, the whole collection of our literature, and the whole fund of observation open to any of us should long since have made evident. Good shelter is a useful good in itself, as shelter. When we try to justify good shelter instead on the pretentious grounds that it will work social

A neighborhood in the city is a place where you can play stickball. (Joe Molnar)

or family miracles we fool ourselves. Reinhold Niebuhr has called this particular self-deception "the doctrine of salvation by bricks."

It is even the same with schools. Important as good schools are, they prove totally undependable at rescuing bad neighborhoods and at creating good neighborhoods. Nor does a good school building guarantee a good education. Schools, like parks, are apt to be volatile creatures of their neighborhoods (as well as being creatures of larger policy). In bad neighborhoods, schools are brought to ruination, physically and socially; while successful neighborhoods improve their schools by fighting for them.*

Nor can we conclude, either, that middle-class families or upper-class families build good neighborhoods, and poor families fail to. For example, within the poverty of the North End in Boston, within the poverty of the West Greenwich Village waterfront neighborhoods, within the poverty of the slaughterhouse district in Chicago (three areas, incidentally, that were all written off as hopeless by their cities' planners), good neighborhoods were created: neighborhoods whose internal problems have grown less with time instead of greater. Meantime, within the once upper-class grace and serenity of Baltimore's beautiful Eutaw Place, within the one-time upper-class solidity of Boston's South End, within the culturally privileged purlieus of New

---

* In the Upper West Side of Manhattan, a badly failed area where social disintegration has been compounded by ruthless bulldozing, project building and shoving people around, annual pupil turnover in schools was more than 50 percent in 1959–60. In 16 schools, it reached an average of 92 percent. It is ludicrous to think that with any amount of effort, official or unofficial, even a tolerable school is possible in a neighborhood of such extreme instability. Good schools are impossible in any unstable neighborhoods with high pupil turnover rates, and this includes unstable neighborhoods which *also* have good housing.

York's Morningside Heights, within miles upon miles of dull, respectable middle-class gray area, bad neighborhoods were created, neighborhoods whose apathy and internal failure grew greater with time instead of less.

To hunt for city neighborhood touchstones of success in high standards of physical facilities, or in supposedly competent nonproblem populations, or in nostalgic memories of town life is a waste of time. It evades the meat of the question, which is the problem of what city neighborhoods do, if anything, that may be socially and economically useful in cities themselves, and how they do it.

We shall have something solid to chew on if we think of city neighborhoods as mundane organs of self-government. Our failures with city neighborhoods are, ultimately, failures in localized self-government. And our successes are successes at localized self-government. I am using self-government in its broadest sense, meaning both the informal and formal self-management of society.

Both the demands on self-government and the techniques for it differ in big cities from the demands and techniques in smaller places. For instance, there is the problem of all those strangers. To think of city neighborhoods as organs of city self-government or self-management, we must first jettison some orthodox but irrelevant notions about neighborhoods which may apply to communities in smaller settlements but not in cities. We must first of all drop any ideal of neighborhoods as self-contained or introverted units.

Unfortunately orthodox planning theory is deeply committed to the ideal of supposedly cozy, inward-

turned city neighborhoods. In its pure form, the
ideal is a neighborhood composed of about 7,000
persons, a unit supposedly of sufficient size to populate an elementary school and to support convenience shopping and a community center. This
unit is then further rationalized into smaller group-
ings of a size scaled to the play and supposed management of children and the chitchat of housewives.
Although the "ideal" is seldom literally reproduced,
it is the point of departure for nearly all neighborhood renewal plans, for all project building, for
much modern zoning, and also for the practice work
done by today's architectural-planning students, who
will be inflicting their adaptations of it on cities to-
morrow. In New York City alone, by 1959, more
than half a million people were already living in
adaptations of this vision of planned neighborhoods.
This "ideal" of the city neighborhood as an island,
turned inward on itself, is an important factor in our
lives nowadays.

   To see why it is a silly and even harmful "ideal"
for cities, we must recognize a basic difference between these concoctions grafted into cities, and town
life. In a town of 5,000 or 10,000 population, if you
go to Main Street (analogous to the consolidated
commercial facilities or community center for a
planned neighborhood), you run into people you
also know at work, or went to school with, or see at
church, or people who are your children's teachers,
or who have sold or given you professional or arti-
san's services, or whom you know to be friends of
your casual acquaintances, or whom you know by
reputation. Within the limits of a town or village,
the connections among its people keep crossing and
recrossing and this can make workable and essentially cohesive communities out of even larger towns

than those of 7,000 population, and to some extent out of little cities.

But a population of 5,000 or 10,000 residents in a big city has no such innate degree of natural cross-connections within itself, except under the most extraordinary circumstances. Nor can city neighbor-hood planning, no matter how cozy in intent, change this fact. If it could, the price would be destruction of a city by converting it into a parcel of towns. As it is, the price of trying, and not even succeeding at a misguided aim, is conversion of a city into a parcel of mutually suspicious and hostile Turfs. There are many other flaws in this "ideal" of the planned neigh-borhood and its various adaptations.*

Lately a few planners, notably Reginald Isaacs of Harvard, have daringly begun to question whether the conception of neighborhood in big cities has any meaning at all. Isaacs points out that city people are mobile. They can and do pick and choose from the entire city (and beyond) for everything from a job, a dentist, recreation, or friends, to shops, entertain-ment, or even in some cases their children's schools.

---

* Even the old reason for settling on an ideal population of about 7,000—sufficient to populate an elementary school—is silly the moment it is applied to big cities, as we discover if we merely ask the question: Which school? In many American cities, paro-chial-school enrollment rivals or surpasses public-school enroll-ment. Does this mean there should be two schools as presumed neighborhood glue, and the population should be twice as large? Or is the population right, and should the schools be half as large? And why the elementary school? If school is to be the touchstone of scale, why not the junior high school, an insti-tution typically far more troublesome in our cities than the ele-mentary school? The question "Which school?" is never asked because this vision is based on no more realism about schools than about anything else. The school is a plausible, and usually abstract, excuse for defining *some* size for a unit that comes out of dreams about imaginary cities. It is necessary as a for-mal framework, to preserve designers from intellectual chaos, and it has no other reason for being. Ebenezer Howard's model towns are the ancestors of the idea, to be sure, but its dura-bility comes from the need to fill an intellectual vacuum.

City people, says Isaacs, are not stuck with the provincialism of a neighborhood, and why should they be? Isn't wide choice and rich opportunity the point of cities?

This is indeed the point of cities. Furthermore, this very fluidity of use and choice among city people is precisely the foundation underlying most city cultural activities and special enterprises of all kinds. Because these can draw skills, materials, customers or clienteles from a great pool, they can exist in extraordinary variety, and not only downtown but in other city districts that develop specialties and characters of their own. And in drawing upon the great pool of the city in this way, city enterprises increase, in turn, the choices available to city people for jobs, goods, entertainment, ideas, contacts, services.

Whatever city neighborhoods may be, or may not be, and whatever usefulness they may have, or may be coaxed into having, their qualities cannot work at cross-purposes to thoroughgoing city mobility and fluidity of *use,* without economically weakening the city of which they are a part. The lack of either economic or social self-containment is natural and necessary to city neighborhoods—simply because they are parts of cities. Isaacs is right when he implies that the conception of neighborhood in cities is meaningless—so long as we think of neighborhoods as being self-contained units to any significant degree, modeled upon town neighborhoods.

But for all the innate extroversion of city neighborhoods, it fails to follow that city people can therefore get along magically without neighborhoods. Even the most urbane citizen does care about the atmosphere of the street and district where he lives, no matter how much choice he has of pursuits outside it; and the common run of city people do depend greatly on their neighborhoods for the kind of everyday lives they lead.

Let us assume (as is often the case) that city neighbors have nothing more fundamental in common with each other than that they share a fragment of geography. Even so, if they fail at managing that fragment decently, the fragment will fail. There exists no inconceivably energetic and all-wise "They" to take over and substitute for localized self-management. Neighborhoods in cities need not supply for their people an artificial town or village life, and to aim at this is both silly and destructive. But neighborhoods in cities do need to supply some means for civilized self-government. This is the problem.

.   .   .

Here is a seeming paradox: To maintain in a neighborhood sufficient people who stay put, a city must have the very fluidity and mobility of use that Reginald Isaacs noted, as mentioned early in this chapter, when he speculated whether neighborhoods can therefore mean anything very significant to cities.

Over intervals of time, many people change their jobs and the locations of their jobs, shift or enlarge their outside friendships and interests, change their family sizes, change their incomes up or down, even change many of their tastes. In short they live, rather than just exist. If they live in diversified, rather than monotonous, districts—in districts, particularly, where many details of physical change can constantly be accommodated—and if they like the place, they can stay put despite changes in the locales or natures of their other pursuits or interests. Unlike the people who must move from a lower-middle to a middle-middle to an upper-middle suburb as their incomes and leisure activities change (or be very outré indeed), or the people of a little town who must move to another town or to a city to find different opportunities, city people need not pull up stakes for such reasons.

A city's collection of opportunities of all kinds, and the fluidity with which these opportunities and choices can be used, is an asset—not a detriment—for encouraging city-neighborhood stability.

However, this asset has to be capitalized upon. It is thrown away where districts are handicapped by sameness and are suitable, therefore, to only a narrow range of incomes, tastes and family circumstances. Neighborhood accommodations for fixed, bodiless, statistical people are accommodations for instability. The people in them, as statistics, may stay the same. But the people in them, as people, do not. Such places are forever way stations. . . .

It is almost beyond imagining that within the very next century a universal city may emerge and that what we now call the country may in fact disappear. Doxiadis, a world-famous city planner, takes a bold look into the future.

8

The Coming Era of Ecumenopolis

by C. A. DOXIADIS

W E must face the fact that modern man has failed to build adequate cities. In the past his problems were simpler, and he solved them by trial and error. Now human forces and mechanical ones are mixed and man is confused. He tries and fails. We say he will become adapted. Yes, he is running the danger of becoming adapted, since adaptation is

From C. A. Doxiadis, "The Coming Era of Ecumenopolis," *Saturday Review*, March 18, 1967. Copyright © 1967 by Saturday Review, Inc. Reprinted by permission of the publisher.

Doxiadis' future cities are already on the drawing boards of many architects throughout the world. Battery Park City will provide office space, apartment houses, shopping centers, and transportation facilities. (Drawing by James Rossant) only meaningful if it means the welfare of man. Prisoners, too, become adapted to conditions! For man to adapt to our present cities would be a mistake, since he is the great prisoner. Not only is man unsafe in his prison, but he is facing a great crisis and heading for disaster.

Confused by the danger, man behaves unwisely. He takes the new conditions of a hostile habitat for granted, and, for example, builds new cities in the image of those that failed or, in the countryside, builds air-conditioned schools with no windows because he is accustomed to doing it in industrial areas. Sometimes he attempts to turn to the past, or dreams of Utopias which have no place in our world. What man needs is an Entopia, an "in-place" which he *can* build, a place which satisfies the dreamer and is acceptable to the scientist, a place where the projections of the artist and the builder merge.

How can man achieve this?

Man and the space surrounding him are connected in many ways within a very complex system. Man's space is just a thin layer on the crust of the earth, consisting of the five elements which shape man and are shaped by him: nature, in which he lives; man himself; society, which he has formed; the shells (or structures) which he builds; and the networks he constructs. This is the real world of man, the *anthropocosmos* halfway between the electron and the universe. But only one subject is of primary importance: man as an individual. The subjects of secondary importance are nature and society. Shells and networks come last. Every element of the anthropocosmos has to serve man; otherwise our endeavor would have no justification.

So how can we best serve our basic subject, man? What is our goal? At this point we have to admit that we have no goals. We are developing a technology that is changing our life, yet we have set no goal for it. No businessman would buy machinery at random when building a factory, no housewife would collect furniture at random for her home. Yet this is exactly what we are doing in the case of our cities, the physical expressions of our life. For them we are producing and collecting at random.

.   .   .

Every individual must feel and be safe, which means that personal safety within a safe society can regulate personal and group conflicts. The question is, at what cost can this be achieved? A man would be much safer if he never left his home, but he wouldn't be happy and he wouldn't develop further. We cannot sacrifice happiness and evolution in the cause of safety, nor safety in the cause of happiness. So we come to the conclusion that what we need is a safety which can guarantee a basis from which to begin our endeavors toward happiness and the fulfillment of our duties to society. This leads to the concept of a system which will allow for different environments offering all degrees of safety, ranging from the absolute one, if possible, for newborn babies and invalids, to a completely natural environment which young people will have to conquer; ranging from sterilized rooms to jungles. In such a habitat we can hope for the best balance between controlled and uncontrolled environment that will offer man the maximum safety and allow the dynamic balance of man and environment which is indispensable for lasting happiness, which is the only goal.

We can now turn to the city of man, but not with preconceived notions about limiting the operation of forces which are independent of man, as people very often do. We must understand that, unlike Utopia, our Entopia depends on forces which are dynamic and which are either uncontrollable or controllable only in the long run. It is these forces which create a new frame for the city to come.

The dynamic forces of developing humanity show that we must be prepared for a continuing increase of population which may well reach 20 to 30 billion people by the end of the next century, at which time it may level off. This will mean a universal city, Ecumenopolis, which will cover the earth with a continuous network of minor and major urban concentrations of different forms. This means that urbanization will continue and that eventually farming may be carried out from urban settlements. This also means that the pressure of population on resources will be such that important measures will have to be taken so that a balance can be retained between the five elements of the anthropocosmos in a universal scale.

But, more than with all separate phenomena, we should be concerned with the survival of man, who, long before the earth has exhausted its capacity for production, will be subjected to great forces pressing him to the point of extinction—forces caused by the elimination of human values in his settlements. If we realize only that at that point the average urban area will have twenty to thirty times more people and a hundred times more machines, and that difficulties grow much faster than the forces causing them, we will understand that this new frame is going to be inhuman in dimensions. If we understand how far the dynamic forces reach, we will see that our real challenge lies not in changing these historical trends —something we cannot do anyway—but in using them for the benefit of man by shaping this universal

city in such a way that not only will it not crush
man, but so that it will provide him with a human
settlement much better than those of today. In order
to do this we have to build the city of inhuman dimensions on the measure of man. We don't have to
invent the human solutions, since they already exist
—we have to understand them and use them within
the new frame.

As an example, a careful study of the cities of the
past proves that the maximum distance from their
centers was ten minutes, and the average one six
minutes, meaning that people walking for a total of
thirty minutes a day could visit the center or other
places two or three times. This shows that there was
a human dimension influencing social and other contacts, and it also gives one example of how it may
be possible to measure a fundamental aspect of the
human city—on the basis of the time dimension and
not that of physical dimensions, since we now have
new means of transportation and communications.

Up to now, measurements in cities have been
based on economic criteria, but these define feasibility more than goals. It is time for man to define goals
and their feasibility at the same time. Man's most
precious commodity, the one which cannot be replaced and which we don't yet know how to expand,
is his own life, which is expressed by its length, or
lifetime. This is the basic commodity as qualified by
the satisfaction and safety man enjoys and as limited by economic considerations, upon which our
formula for the city will have to be based.

Man, in this case the average American citizen,
spends 76 per cent of his lifetime at home (males
69 per cent and females 83 per cent), and 24 per
cent away from it. He spends 36 per cent sleeping,

20 per cent working, and 10 per cent eating, dressing, and bathing. He is left with 34 per cent, or one-third of his life, for leisure, pleasure, thought, etc. It is this one-third which constitutes the basic difference between man and animal. But males ages twenty to fifty-nine have only 20 per cent of free time, of which one-third is spent in commuting. This means ninety minutes; but for some people it means three hours, or two-thirds of their free time.

On the basis of such calculations we can develop a time budget, which is more important than any other budget for man, and estimate how much time each man can afford to spend on each of his activities. We can then qualify the satisfaction that man gets at every time length. Is it better for him, for example, to walk for twenty minutes, drive in a Volkswagen for ten, or in a Cadillac for two hours? We can also try to measure the degree of safety at every time length. In principle, then, total satisfaction would be the product of time multiplied by satisfaction. A happy life would be the product of time multiplied by satisfaction multiplied by safety. If we now insert into the picture the factor of economic feasibility for satisfaction, we have the formula of feasible happiness, which is leading to the human city that we can build, our common Entopia which should include all our personal Entopias in a balanced whole, the Entopia which is the common denominator of our feasible dreams.

If we have managed to define human man, natural happiness, and reasonable safety, and measure them, we can define the human city. It will be very big, but it will consist of two categories of parts, the cells and the networks. The cells are going to be the size of the cities of the past—no larger than 50,000 inhabitants, no larger than 2,000 by 2,000 yards, no larger than a ten-minute average walk. They will be built on a human scale on the basis of human experience. The networks are going to be absolutely mechanical and automatic, interconnecting the cells by transportation and communications, forming enormous organisms with the cells as basic units. Their vehicles will reach speeds of many hundreds of miles an hour; their arteries will be underground, not highways but deepways, as they are in the bodies of all mammals. The higher the speed the deeper they will go. In the cells man will be offered all choices, from isolation and solitude to very intense participation in social and political life. (The fact that we need TV should not lead us to the elimination of the marketplace. We don't need only one-way communications, we need a natural human dialogue as well.)

The surface of the city will allow the flora to spread again, beginning from small gardens within the cells, to major zones of forests above the tunnels of the networks, to big farming areas and natural reserves where man will find the rough conditions which he also needs. Society will operate much more efficiently, and people will come together in a multitude of both natural and artificial ways.

Houses will be the natural environment, not formally specified, since there the individual will want to express himself. Normal multi-story residence buildings will need much greater areas per floor so that a whole community will be able to operate at each level—a community with its shopping center, playgrounds, and public squares. Automated factories will be placed within the earth, especially in hills and mountains.

Man will be free to move over the surface of the whole city, and even though the buildings will be as pleasant as possible, he will have many chances of walking or staying out without shelter or protection, since his whole organism must be kept fit for all sorts of adjustments that the future may necessitate. In this city we can hope that man, relieved of all stresses that arise from his conflict with the machine, will allow his body to dance, his senses to express themselves through the arts, his mind to dedicate itself to philosophy or mathematics, and his soul to love and to dream.

It has often been said that man may exterminate himself through science. What we must also say is that man's hopes for a much better evolution lie in science, which, after all, is the only acquisition of a proved universal value that he can transmit from generation to generation. The whole difference between extermination and evolution lies in the goal that science will set.

The task is hard. People must learn to recognize that they must be very conservative when dealing with man, and very revolutionary when dealing with new systems and networks. The task is also hard because many expect magical solutions overnight, or formulas for the immediate solution of the problems. They actually like to talk about sufferings, and they do not understand that cities face such acute problems because man does not have a system of values with which to define what a good life is. Personally, I am convinced that the root of all problems in our cities lies in our minds, in our loss of belief in man and in his ability to set goals and to implement them.

We can never solve problems and tackle diseases unless we conceive the whole. We cannot build a cathedral by carving stones but only by dreaming of it, conceiving it as a whole, developing a systematic approach, and only then working out the details. But dreaming and conceiving are not enough. We have to carve the stones and lift them.

One of the great cities of the ancient
world is here described by the Greek
historian Herodotus (484–425 B.C.). At
the time when he wrote this selection,
Babylon was already an ancient ruin.

9

Ancient Babylon

by HERODOTUS

THERE are in Assyria many other great cities; but
the most famous and the strongest was Babylon, where the royal dwelling had been set after the
destruction of Ninus. Babylon was a city such as I
will now describe. It lies in a great plain, and is in
shape a square, each side an hundred and twenty

From *Herodotus* (Vol. I), tr. A. D. Godley (Cambridge, Mass.:
Harvard University Press, 1921), pp. 221–227. Reprinted by permission of the Loeb Classical Library.

furlongs in length; thus four hundred and eighty
furlongs make the complete circuit of the city. Such
is the size of the city of Babylon; and it was planned
like no other city whereof we know. Round it runs
first a fosse deep and wide and full of water, and
then a wall of fifty royal cubits' thickness and two
hundred cubits' height. The royal cubit is greater
by three fingers' breadth than the common cubit.

Further, I must show where the earth was used
as it was taken from the fosse and in what manner
the wall was wrought. As they dug the fosse, they
made bricks of the earth which was carried out of the
place they dug, and when they had moulded bricks
enough they baked them in ovens; then using hot
bitumen for cement and interposing layers of
wattled reeds at every thirtieth course of bricks,
they built first the border of the fosse and then the
wall itself in the same fashion. On the top, along
the edges of the wall, they built houses of a single
chamber, facing each other, with space enough between for the driving of a four-horse chariot. There
are a hundred gates in the circle of the wall, all of
bronze, with posts and lintels of the same. There is
another city, called Is, eight days' journey from

Babylon, where is a little river, also named Is, a
tributary stream of the river Euphrates; from the
source of this river the bitumen was brought for the
wall of Babylon.

Thus then was this wall built; the city is divided
into two parts; for it is cut in half by a river named
Euphrates, a wide, deep, and swift river. The ends of
the wall, then, on either side are built quite down to
the river; here they turn, and hence a fence of baked
bricks runs along each bank of the stream. The city
itself is full of houses three and four stories high;
and the ways which traverse it—those that run cross-
wise towards the river, and the rest—are all straight.
Further, at the end of each road there was a gate in
the riverside fence, one gate for each alley; these
gates also were of bronze, and these too opened on
the river.

These walls are the city's outer armour; within
them there is another encircling wall, well nigh as
strong as the other, but narrower. In the mid-most
of one division of the city stands the royal palace,
surrounded by a high and strong wall; and in the
mid-most of the other is still to this day the sacred
enclosure of Zeus Belus, a square of two furlongs
each way, with gates of bronze. In the center of
this enclosure a solid tower has been built, of one
furlong's length and breadth; a second tower rises
from this, and from it yet another, till at last there
are eight. The way up to them mounts spirally outside all the towers; about halfway in the ascent is a
halting place, with seats for repose, where those

who ascend sit down and rest. In the last tower there is a great shrine; and in it a great and well-covered couch is laid and a golden table set hard by.

In 1519, Hernando Cortes, an adventurer
from the Spanish Court, entered Tenochtitlán (now Mexico City) and captured
the Aztec ruler, Montezuma. In this
letter to King Charles V, he wrote of
the magnificence of the city even when
compared with the greatest cities in
Spain.

10

Mexico City in
Montezuma's Time

by HERNANDO CORTES

THIS city has many public squares, in which are
situated the markets and other places for buying and selling. There is one square twice as large as
that of the city of Salamanca, surrounded by porti-
cos, where are daily assembled more than sixty
thousand souls, engaged in buying and selling, and

From Hernando Cortes, *Despatches to Emperor Charles V*
(New York, 1843), pp. 112–114.

These piñatas testify that the markets of modern-day Mexico are just as festive and colorful as those of ancient Tenochtitlán. (Braniff International)

where are found all kinds of merchandise that the
world affords, embracing the necessaries of life, as
for instance articles of food, as well as jewels of gold
and silver, lead, brass, copper, tin, precious stones,
bone, shells, snails, and feathers. There are also exposed for sale wrought and unwrought stone, bricks
burnt and unburnt, timber hewn and unhewn, of
different sorts. There is a street for game, where
every variety of birds found in the country are sold,
as fowls, partridges, quails, wild ducks, fly-catchers,
widgeons, turtle-doves, pigeons, reedbirds, parrots,
sparrows, eagles, hawks, owls, and kestrels; they sell
likewise the skins of some birds of prey, with their
feathers, head, beak, and claws. There are also sold
rabbits, hares, deer, and little dogs, which are raised
for eating. There is also an herb street, where may be
obtained all sorts of roots and medicinal herbs that
the country affords. There are apothecaries' shops,
where prepared medicines, liquids, ointments, and
plasters are sold; barbers' shops, where they wash
and shave the head; and restaurateurs, that furnish
food and drink at a certain price. There is also a
class of men like those called in Castile porters, for
carrying burthens. Wood and coals are seen in
abundance, and braziers of earthenware for burn-
ing coals; mats of various kinds for beds, others of
a lighter sort for seats, and for halls and bedrooms.
There are all kinds of green vegetables, especially
onions, leeks, garlic, watercress, nasturtium, borage,
sorrel, artichokes, and golden thistle; fruits also of
numerous descriptions, amongst which are cherries
and plums, similar to those in Spain; honey and

wax from bees, and from the stalks of maize, which are as sweet as the sugar-cane; honey is also extracted from the plant called maguey, which is superior to sweet or new wine; from the same plant they extract sugar and wine, which they also sell. Different kinds of cotton thread of all colors in skeins are exposed for sale in one quarter of the market, which has the appearance of the silk-market at Granada, although the former is supplied more abundantly. Painters' colors, as numerous as can be found in Spain, and as fine shades; deerskins dressed and undressed, dyed different colors; earthenware of a large size and excellent quality; large and small jars, jugs, pots, bricks, and an endless variety of vessels, all made of fine clay, and all or most of them glazed and painted; maize, or Indian corn, in the grain and in the form of bread, preferred in the grain for its flavor to that of the other islands; pâtés of birds and fish; great quantities of fish, fresh, salt, cooked and uncooked; the eggs of hens, geese, and of all the other birds I have mentioned, in great abundance, and cakes made of eggs; finally, everything that can be found throughout the whole country is sold in the markets, comprising articles so numerous that to avoid prolixity, and because their names are not retained in my memory, or are unknown to me, I shall not attempt to enumerate them. Every kind of merchandise is sold in a particular street or quarter assigned to it exclusively, and thus the best order is preserved. They sell everything by number or measure; at least so far we have not observed them to sell anything by weight. There is a building in the great square that is used as an audience house, where ten or twelve persons, who are magistrates, sit and decide all controversies that arise in the market, and order delinquents to be punished. In the same square there are other persons who go constantly about among the people observing what is sold, and the measures used in selling; and they have been seen to break measures that were not true.

Few cities have as dynamic a history as that of the second largest city in the United States. From mud hole to commercial giant, from Slab Town to cultural center, this is the story of Chicago.

11

Chicago—
The Young Giant

by WILLIAM E. WOODWARD

For about four decades of the last century—from 1840 until well into the 1880's—Chicago grew more rapidly in population and in commercial importance than any other community in the world. It was like a hearty lad who outgrows his clothes before he has had time to get used to them. One

From W. E. Woodward, *The Way Our People Lived* (New York: Washington Square Press, 1968), pp. 260–263. Copyright 1944 by William E. Woodward. Reprinted by permission of Liveright Publishers, New York.

strange feature of this button-bursting expansion is that the site of Chicago was about the last place along the shore of Lake Michigan where one might reasonably expect the birth of a metropolis. The town stood at the mouth of the Chicago River, which at that time was too shallow for navigation. The land was low, wet and malarial. The ground on which the city's principal business section stands— now known as the Loop—was a marsh only a few inches higher than the level of the lake.

In 1837 the Illinois legislature had incorporated the community as a city under the name of Chicago, an Anglicized Indian word supposed to mean the smell of wild onions. But there is some doubt over the meaning. In the speech of the Pottawottomies there is a word that sounds as if it might be spelled *chickagou*. It is said to mean "stench," but linguists skilled in Indian lore assert that an almost identical word in the Chippewa idiom means "apple blossoms." So you may take your choice, though it is a matter of small importance.

Its name in popular speech was Slab Town, and so it was known far and wide. It was called Slab Town because every house in the community was a hastily flung-together, boxlike structure of boards or split logs. Besides Chicago and Slab Town the place had still another name, evolved from the experiences of strangers who had unwittingly tried to dash across a street in rainy weather. By them it was called the Mud Hole of the Prairies, a descriptive term that was devised to convey a sense of opprobrium and disapproval. But it failed completely to have any effect on the inhabitants of Slab Town, for they were as accustomed to mud as a bird to the air.

The new little city had a population of about 4,000, made up chiefly of fur traders, grain buyers,

wagoners, blacksmiths, gamblers and shopkeepers—
as well as a lot of idle adventurers, ready for anything
except hard work. In manner or deportment its
residents were like those of the other new towns of
the Middle West. They drank their tumblers of raw
whisky, gambled excessively, danced all night,
whooped and yelled and fired guns and pistols frequently, with or without adequate incentive. Murders occurred too often to attract much attention.

But neither mud nor murders held Chicago down.
In 1857, twenty years after its incorporation, the
city had 93,000 inhabitants and newcomers were still
arriving in an unbroken stream. It had ten first-class
hotels—among them the Tremont, a four-story
brick structure—besides forty-odd hostelries of lower degree. There were a dozen banks, forty newspapers and periodicals of various kinds, and fifteen
hundred business establishments. It was the terminus
of eleven trunk line railroads, and more than one
hundred trains arrived or departed every day.

It was no longer called Slab Town but the derisive
name of Mud Hole of the Prairies still remained.
After every rain the black prairie soil became a vast
mud puddle, with shallow ponds of muddy water
standing in the streets.

In 1855 engineers and drainage experts who had
studied the situation concluded that the only prac-
ticable solution was to raise the whole area twelve
feet above the level of the lake by covering it with
fresh soil.

It was a prodigious undertaking, and Chicago
tackled it with the energy of muscular youth. Two
square miles of land—streets, gardens, lawns and
backyards—were eventually covered with earth
sucked up from the bed of the river, for a channel-
deepening job was going on at the same time. It was

This is an aerial view of downtown Chicago. Today Chicago is just as bustling as it ever was, but it has become much more modern. (American Airlines)

a task beset by extraordinary difficulties. For one thing, street traffic had to go on while the streets were being lifted. Thousands of buildings had to be brought up to the street level.

The Tremont Hotel, built of brick, was the largest building in the city. It was nearly two hundred feet long and four stories tall. Engineers thought this huge structure could be lifted, but they thought it would cause so many cracks, fissures, floors askew, tilted ceilings and doors out of line with their frames, that, after the job was over, the hotel would have to be almost wholly rebuilt. While the owners of the Tremont were wondering what to do the street in front of the hotel had been raised and when guests arrived they walked down a flight of wooden steps to the hotel office.

The proprietors of the hotel were about ready to tear down the building when a young man of twenty-seven—named George M. Pullman—appeared on the scene. He was a building contractor from the East, where he had heard of the Tremont and the problem of raising it. After looking over the structure he declared that he could lift it without disturbing a teaspoon in a coffee cup or breaking even one pane of glass. In desperation they gave him the contract. He employed twelve hundred workmen and used five thousand jackscrews placed at regular intervals in the basement of the hotel. Upon a signal every workman gave the lever of a set of jackscrews half a turn. The enormously heavy building rose, an inch at a time, to the street level. There was no damage done and none of the guests was disturbed by the operation.

George M. Pullman remained in Chicago. His name is world-famous; he was the creator of the Pullman sleeping car.

"Its streets were mud sloughs, its sidewalks a series of more or less rotten planks," wrote Charles Dudley Warner, in his remembrances of Chicago, where he had lived and practiced law until 1860. "Half the town was in process of elevation above the tadpole level and a considerable part on wheels —a moving house being about the only wheeled vehicle that could get around with any comfort to the passengers."

Nothing could stop the rushing progress of the wonder city of the Midwest. By 1870 its population had grown up to 300,000. Farms on the prairie were surrounded and swallowed by the advancing city, and poor farmers, to their own amazement, found themselves rich from the sale of their land. As a meat-packing center Chicago had passed Cincinnati. Seventeen huge grain elevators, with a capacity of twelve million bushels, raised their tall heads alongside the freight yards. Chicago wholesale houses had become the largest of their kind, and their salesmen were to be found traveling all over the Western states, selling goods to a legion of retail merchants.

Stone sidewalks had been laid in the downtown business section, but the rest of the city—even in the wealthy districts—still tripped along on planks. A huge sewage system had been established; it had only one serious fault—it wouldn't work. On the lake shore rose the palatial homes of the new-rich; some of them were marble palaces. Along the Chicago River, and north, west and south were the homes of the laboring poor; some of them were muddy hovels, made of rough boards.

The city was always full of strangers who had come to better their fortunes, or to escape the consequences of their misdeeds, or to avoid their creditors. But there were also many decent workmen who hoped to obtain work in a railroad shop or an industrial plant, for Chicago employers were said to pay higher wages than those prevailing in the East. The boisterous city of glamour and mud, easy fortunes and loose spending, also attracted a swarm of gamblers and plausible swindlers.

Young men who were just beginning their careers, or who had not been able to find a place for themselves at home, were probably the most numerous of all the newcomers. . . .

Mark Twain, America's foremost story-teller, presents his picture of New Orleans on his return to the city in 1883, after a number of years had passed. His opinionated views of this southern city range from "waste-paper-littered" to "deep, warm, and vari-colored."

12

New Orleans in the 1880's

by MARK TWAIN

THE city itself had not changed—to the eye. It had greatly increased in spread and population, but the look of the town was not altered. The dust, waste-paper-littered, was still deep in the streets; the deep troughlike gutters along the curb-stones were still half full of reposeful water with a

From Mark Twain, *Life on the Mississippi* (1883), quoted in *Travels with Mark Twain*, ed. Charles Neider (New York: Coward McCann, 1961), pp. 128–131. Reprinted by permission of Harper & Row, Publishers.

Modern New Orleans has just as many problems as the New Orleans of the 1880's described by Mark Twain. (Paul Conklin-OEO)

dusty surface; the sidewalks were still in the sugar and bacon region—encumbered by casks and barrels and hogsheads; the great blocks of austerely plain commercial houses were as dusty-looking as ever.

Canal Street was finer and more attractive and stirring than formerly, with its drifting crowds of people, its several processions of hurrying streetcars, and—toward evening—its broad second-story verandas crowded with gentlemen and ladies clothed according to the latest mode.

Not that there is any architecture in Canal Street; to speak in broad, general terms, there is no architecture in New Orleans, except in the cemeteries. It seems a strange thing to say of a wealthy, far-seeing, and energetic city of a quarter of a million inhabitants, but it is true. There is a huge granite

United States custom-house—costly enough, genuine enough, but as to decoration it is inferior to a gasometer. It looks like a state prison. But it was built before the war. Architecture in America may be said to have been born since the war. New Orleans, I believe, has had the good luck—and in a sense the bad luck—to have had no great fire in late years. It must be so. If the opposite had been the case, I think one would be able to tell the "burnt district" by the radical improvement in its architecture over the old forms. One can do this in Boston and Chicago. The "burnt district" of Boston was commonplace before the fire; but now there is no commercial district in any city in the world that can surpass it—or perhaps even rival it—in beauty, elegance, and tastefulness.

However, New Orleans has begun—just this moment, as one may say. When completed, the new Cotton Exchange will be a stately and beautiful building: massive, substantial, full of architectural graces; no shams or false pretenses or uglinesses about it anywhere. To the city it will be worth many times its cost, for it will breed its specie. What has been lacking hitherto was a model to build toward, something to educate eye and taste: a suggester, so to speak.

The city is well outfitted with progressive men—thinking, sagacious, long-headed men. The contrast between the spirit of the city and the city's architecture is like the contrast between waking and sleep.

Apparently there is a "boom" in everything but that one dead feature. The water in the gutters used to be stagnant and slimy, and a potent disease-breeder; but the gutters are flushed now two or three times a day by powerful machinery; in many of the gutters the water never stands still, but has a steady current. Other sanitary improvements have been made; and with such effect that New Orleans claims to be (during the long intervals between the occasional yellow-fever assaults) one of the healthiest cities in the Union. There's plenty of ice now for everybody, manufactured in the town. It is a driving place commercially, and has a great river, ocean, and railway business. At the date of our visit it was the best-lighted city in the Union, electrically speaking. The New Orleans electric lights were more numerous than those of New York, and very much better. One had this modified noonday not only in Canal and some neighboring chief streets, but all along a stretch of five miles of river-frontage. There are good clubs in the city now—several of them but recently organized—and inviting modern-style pleasure resorts at West End and Spanish Fort. The telephone is everywhere. One of the most notable advances is in journalism. The newspapers, as I remember them, were not a striking feature. Now they are. Money is spent upon them with a free hand. They get the news, let it cost what it may. The editorial work is not hack-grinding, but literature. As an example of New Orleans journalistic achievement, it may be mentioned that the *Times-Democrat* of August 26, 1882, contained a report of the year's business of the towns of the Mississippi Valley, from New Orleans all the way to St. Paul—two thousand miles. That issue of the paper consisted of forty pages; seven columns to the page;

two hundred and eighty columns in all; fifteen hundred words to the column; an aggregate of four hundred and twenty thousand words. That is to say, not much short of three times as many words as are in this book. One may with sorrow contrast this with the architecture of New Orleans.

I have been speaking of public architecture only. The domestic article in New Orleans is reproachless, notwithstanding it remains as it always was. All the dwellings are of wood in the American part of the town, I mean—and all have a comfortable look. Those in the wealthy quarter are spacious; painted snow-white usually, and generally have wide verandas, or double verandas, supported by ornamental columns. These mansions stand in the center of large grounds, and rise, garlanded with roses, out of the midst of swelling masses of shining green foliage and many-colored blossoms. No houses could well be in better harmony with their surroundings, or more pleasing to the eye, or more homelike and comfortable-looking.

One even becomes reconciled to the cistern presently; this is a mighty cask, painted green, and sometimes a couple of stories high, which is propped against the house-corner on stilts. There is a mansion-and-brewery suggestion about the combination which seems very incongruous at first. But the people cannot have wells, and so they take rain-water. Neither can they conveniently have cellars or graves, the town being built upon "made" ground;

The French quarter with its iron-railed verandas is still the most colorful .section of modern New Orleans. (Pan Am)

so they do without both, and few of the living complain, and none of the others.

The old French part of New Orleans—anciently the Spanish part—bears no resemblance to the American end of the city; the American end which lies beyond the intervening brick business center. The houses are massed in blocks; are austerely plain and dignified; uniform of pattern, with here and there a departure from it with pleasant effect; all are plastered on the outside, and nearly all have long, iron-railed verandas running along the several stories. Their chief beauty is the deep, warm, vari-colored stain with which time and the weather have enriched the plaster. It harmonizes with all the surroundings and has as natural a look of belonging there as has the flush upon sunset clouds. This charming decoration cannot be successfully imitated; neither is it to be found elsewhere in America.

Here the author describes in vivid detail his observations of post-World War II Tokyo, the world's most populous city. People, cultural variety, and constant movement make this city unique.

13

Tokyo, in the 1950's

by FOSCO MARAINI

THE fascination of Tokyo, the crossroads of the world, lies in its taste for life, however confused and disoriented it may be. "Chicago," it has been said, "is stupefying . . . an incomprehensible phenomenon. . . ."* All that, and more, could be

* J. Street, quoted by J. Gunther, *Inside U.S.A.* (New York, 1947).

From Fosco Maraini, *Meeting with Japan* (New York: The Viking Press, 1960), pp. 38–41. Copyright © 1959 by Hutchinson and Company (Publishers) Ltd., London. Reprinted by permission of The Viking Press, Inc., and Hutchinson and Company (Publishers) Ltd.

said of Tokyo. Chicago is, after all, the product of a single civilization, that of the West. But here we are confronted with a world synthesis. Here there meet and mingle the twenty-six civilizations of Toynbee, the eighteen religions, the five kalpas (Buddhist cosmic eras), the thirty-eight races and sub-races of mankind, the seventy styles of cooking, the six perfumes, the eighty-two smells, the 120,000 stinks, the twelve dozen kinds of dirt, the seven wonders, the thousand lights, the 2,600 tongues. Not for nothing has another American called it a "wonderful, hybrid, dissolute, noisy, quiet, brooding, garish, simpering, silly, contemplative, cultured, absurd city."*

Nowhere else in the world can you see in the streets girls and women in kimonos, either vividly coloured or subdued according to their age, young women in Paris models, girls in jeans, or Indian saris, or neat Chinese dresses; mothers leading their children by the hand, or carrying them on their back, or pushing them in prams; men in shirts, in work happi, in the uniform of ten different armies, with their sons on their back, in straw sandals, gumboots, overalls, eighth-century costume, in shorts, rags, smart white suits, in yukata, in haori hakama and bowler hats, or in montsuki; with black, red, or fair hair; with almond shaped eyes or blue eyes; men who drag their feet (Japanese), gesticulate (Latins), walk stiffly and inexorably (Teutons) or loosely and smilingly (Americans); huge men with long hair knotted on top of their

---

* O. D. Russell, *Here's Tokyo* (Tokyo, 1953).

Hustle and bustle are the bywords of downtown Tokyo. Here East and West meet in an exciting atmosphere of tradition and change. (BOAC)

heads (sumo wrestlers), martial and agile Sikhs
in pink turbans, human relics of Hiroshima or
Nagasaki; white-shirted disabled ex-servicemen beg-
ging and pathetically playing some instrument while
the victors pass with girls on their arms; boys on
bicycles demonstrating their virtuosity by threading
their way through the traffic with one hand on the
handlebar and the other holding aloft two or three
layers of trays full of food; men-horses pulling per-
fumed, heavily made-up geishas; people terrified
of infection wearing surgeon's masks over their
faces; students in uniform, railwaymen in uniform,
postmen in uniform, firemen in uniform, nurses in
uniform; itinerant fluteplayers who hide their heads
in baskets; men disguised as insects or corpses who
dance, cut capers, or beat drums or do whatever else
may be required to advertise some product or other;
sellers of red-fish, or of roasted sweet potatoes, or
a special bean paste made up in beautiful wooden
boxes; baseball players returning from a game; pipe-
cleaners pushing carts on which a tiny kettle is per-
petually whistling; Coca-Cola sellers wearing the
uniform and device of the firm; masseurs, who are
generally blind; aged widows with their hair cut
short; Buddhist nuns with shaved heads; scowling
colonels of the reserve in kimono and bowler hat.

Only here do you see signs in so many different
languages. Roman characters are often used with

curious results, such as "flolist" for "florist," or "dearer" for "dealer," because the Japanese have difficulty in distinguishing "l" from "r." "Long 'r' or short 'r'?" is the question that they continually ask when trying to write down a western name. Once upon a time extraordinary things were to be seen, such as the sign "Ladies have fits upstairs" outside a tailor's, or "Every client promptly executed" outside a barber's. Now, however, linguistic knowledge has progressed.

Nowhere else but in Tokyo are there to be seen in the shop windows dwarf trees 200 years old, as twisted and strange as the 1,000-year-old giants of the forest, growing in tiny porcelain pots; ancient lacquer boxes, exquisitely decorated with pictures in gold, formerly used for keeping medicines, side by side with high precision optical instruments . . . or the latest models of the American, European, and Japanese motor industries; displays of sandals for men and women, umbrellas made of paper and bamboo, wigs for wives or geishas, stone lanterns, stamps with complicated ideograms, side by side with typewriters, refrigerators, wireless sets, calculating machines, cultivated pearls, plastic goods, travel agencies; big department stores—Mitsukoshi, Takashimaya, Matusuya, Shirokiya, Matsuzakaya—where you can buy anything from four ounces of seaweed for your evening meal to a yacht for your next summer's cruise—stand cheek by jowl with the tiny shops of craftsmen each specializing in one single article, which he often makes himself with the aid of his family, using agile fingers which have inherited the skill of many generations. A kampo-gaku-ya, the hair-raising, sinister, old-fashioned,

"Chinese-style" chemist's shop, displays in the window mummified snakes, asps, vipers, tortoises, monkeys, big bottles of yellow liquid containing terrifying worms that look like embryonic dragons, while next door the modern Japanese chemical industry is busy manufacturing for the markets of Asia every new synthetic product.

From the beginning of its existence as a Portuguese colony in the sixteenth century, Brazil has been in search of a capital (Bahia, Rio de Janeiro, Brasilia). John Dos Passos, a famous American novelist, discusses his trip to this new capital, which was first carved out of the highlands of central Brazil in 1956.

14

Brasilia

by JOHN DOS PASSOS

THE Brasilia Palace Hotel was almost complete. Comfortable beds, airy rooms. Hot and cold water, electric light. To be sure the silence of the plateau was broken at night by the sound of hammering and sawing on the annex they are building out back and by the swish of shovels of men at work spreading soil for a garden between the res-

From John Dos Passos, *Brazil on the Move* (New York: Doubleday & Company, 1963), pp. 76–79. Copyright © 1963 by John Dos Passos. Reprinted by permission of the author.

taurant's glass wall and the curving edges of the
tiled swimming pool.

Niemeyer's   strange mania   for underground
entrances has saddled the hotel with an unneces-
sarily inconvenient lobby. It surprised us to find so
little regard for the necessary functions of a building.
In case of fire, we asked each other, how would we
ever get out?

The presidential palace we found to be a sin-
gularly beautiful building of glass and white con-
crete, built long and low to fit into the long lines
of the hills on the horizon, floating as lightly as a
flock of swans on broad mirroring pools of clear
water that flanked the entrance. The inner partitions
were glass too. We did ask each other where, amid
all those glass walls, the poor President could find
a spot to change his trousers or a private nook to
write a letter in.

From the palace we drove on a wide highway to
what was to correspond to Capitol Hill in Washington: The Triangle of the Three Powers they
called it. An enormous open space. Draglines were
leveling the red clay hills. Drills, like gigantic cork-
screws, were boring for the foundation piling. Here
would rise the circular halls for the Senate and
House and a pair of . . . steel and glass buildings
behind to house their offices. These would be
balanced by a building for the Supreme Court and
another for the executive departments. From there
a broad mall with many roadways would run between rows of ministries to the downtown center
where the banks and the hotels and the theaters and

Brazil's third capital, Brasilia, was built from scratch in the central part of the country. Its modern Senate and Congress Buildings take a leap forward into the twenty-first century. (Pan Am)

the department stores were to be established. From this center, "like the wings of a jet plane," were to stretch in either direction blocks of apartment buildings and private residences. To form the tail of the plane a continuation of the mall would stretch for miles in the direction of the eventual railroad station and the industrial suburbs.

There was not to be a traffic light in the city. Every intersection was to be by overpass or underpass. Unobstructed roadways would feed the traffic into the center of each block where ample parking space was foreseen under the open understories of the buildings. Automobile traffic would come in from the rear. The front of every apartment building or private house was to open on a landscaped square. Shopping centers on the North American suburban plan were to be built within walking distance of each residential block so that the paths for pedestrians would be separate from the automobile roads.

We found ourselves imagining the buildings to be, the great paved spaces, the lawns and gardens, the serried louvers and trellises shading the windows from the sun, the gleaming walls of tile and glass.

"This is the underground bus terminal," said [the head of the building corporation], patting a wall of smooth red clay affectionately with his hand. "Escalators will take people up to the great paved central platform above. . . . To the left is the theater and restaurant district . . . a little Montmartre."

He burst into his creaky laugh. "Of course you think we're mad. A man has to be a little mad to get anything accomplished in Brazil."

His quarrel with his American engineers, he began to explain, was that they were not mad enough. They were helpful and practical but they were so accustomed to perfect machinery they had forgotten how to improvise. "In the old days you Americans were the greatest improvisers in the world." In Brazil everything had to be improvised.

He went on to tell one of his favorite stories. Once when he was running the Rio Doce Company a flood took the piers out from under a steel bridge.

Traffic stopped. If the ore stopped going out, the dollars stopped coming in. His American engineers said they could repair the bridge all right but they'd have to wait for a crane to come from the States. That crane would have taken months even if he'd had the dollars to buy it. Among the work gangs he found a gigantic Negro who said he knew how to get the bridge back on its piers without a crane. . . .

I'd seen the great oxen in the Rio Doce? I nodded. Yes, I'd seen eleven yokes hitched together. How could one forget the great teams of oxen straining forward with the pondered magnificence of a frieze on an early Greek temple? . . .

Well, he went on excitedly, with a hundred oxen and levers and jacks and winches that illiterate Negro had the bridge open for traffic in nineteen days. . . . "Improvise . . . that is my answer when people tell me that trying to build a capital out here on the plateau is a crazy project. . . . Central Brazil must have roads, it must have buildings . . . out of sheer necessity we are improvising Brasilia."

New Towns, like Reston, represent creative attempts to build small cities that will provide more pleasurable living for their inhabitants while at the same time relieving the population pressure of the large cities.

15

Reston, Virginia: A New Town

by ERVIN GALANTAY

L AST summer I was sitting on Lake Anne Plaza, enjoying my drink and taking stock of the visual elements that provide a complete pattern book for urban designers. The space was well used. Handsome young people passed, entered shops or pulled boats along the basin. Chairs under umbrellas were filled with tourists, including Washington bureaucrats entertaining minor foreign statesmen. It seemed

Condensed from Ervin Galantay, "Architecture," *The Nation*, December 12, 1966, by permission of *The Nation*.

Reston, Virginia. High-rise apartments and cafés contribute to Reston's pleasurable living. (William Graham—Conklin and Rossant, architects)

incredible that all this activity could occur in the center of a village with an actual population of little more than 1,000 people. Seeing my notes, a jovial man came up and introduced himself as a builder who was putting up a "regular kind" of subdivision not far from Reston. He wanted to know whether I intended to buy a home in the area. In return I asked him what he thought of Reston. He confided that he comes mainly to check on Simon's sales. The architecture made him uncomfortable. "Disneyland," he said, "Simon's folly." I countered that children would be happier in Disneyland than in Levittown. He remained unimpressed. "You can't build more than one such place around here. Simon has captured the entire screwball market," and there can be no demand for another such town since most people want the familiar split levels, ranches, colonials. People who want Europe can take a trip. I wondered whether it had ever occurred to him that people "want" the usual suburb because they have been shown little else. Thus the pioneer deed of Reston may be to expose visitors to a mode of living where buildings are closely clustered to leave generous expanses for recreation, instead of the monotonous spread of identical lots.

Apparently many people think of the New Towns as a newfangled and imported fad like miniskirts and Beatles. Yet the idea has a venerable lineage: New Town policies were practiced in imperial Rome and imperial China, in medieval Europe, as well as in the Americas, until the frontier was settled. In fact, interest in New Towns shows a cyclic pattern and we seem to be approaching the zenith once more, after a slow rise since Ebenezer Howard's "Garden City" proposals of 1902. Although the United States leads in the world phenomenon of suburbanization it lags in the development of wholly planned New Towns, being outdistanced not only by Great Britain, Sweden and France but also by the Eastern bloc countries. The USSR alone has built more than 800 New Towns, four of which have already grown to populations beyond half a million. Unlike their European counterparts the American New Towns are built by private enterprise. There are in the country at present fifty to seventy-five totally planned communities in some stage of design or construction, but few of them would qualify as New Towns as the term is currently understood. Ideally, New Towns are balanced communities that provide jobs for the job holders who will live in them, although some commuting in and out of town is acceptable. Among U.S. developers 6,000 acres seem to mark the limit between a large subdivision and a New Town, and this corresponds to a population of between 60,000 and 100,000 people. The optimal size of such communities is constantly re-evaluated, generally upward. In 1902 Howard considered 32,000 inhabitants the ceiling, but today this is thought far too small a group to support basic facilities like a college or hospital. No less than 100,000 people may be needed to sustain a culturally self-contained New Town, although some planners still favor smaller communities. Constantinos Doxiadis, the most influential Greek urbanist since Hippodamus of Miletus, prefers 50,000 people and argues for a complex of only 1,000 acres, the center of which can be reached on foot from any point within ten minutes—as in most historic towns. By comparison, the largest American New Town, Irvine Ranch in California, will spread over 93,000 acres.

In the United States the most rewarding area for the study of New Towns is the Washington-Baltimore conurbation, where at least four can be found in advanced stages of planning or development. The area is one of the fastest growing in the nation, but credit must also be given to Washington's "Year

2000" plan, which proposed an orderly pattern for the growth of the capital along radial corridors separated by green "wedges" and actually pinpointed the desirable locations for New Towns. Among these, Reston enjoys the publicity advantages of a head start, but already its architects, Whittlesey, Conklin and Rossant, are working on plans for a second venture near Germantown. On the same "corridor" as Germantown, the Baltimore firm of Rogers, Taliaferro, Kostritski & Lamb is building Montgomery Village, named thus modestly because it will accommodate only some 35,000 people. The most interesting social experiments are being pursued in the creation of the New Town of Columbia, halfway between Washington and Baltimore, and planned by the Community Research, Inc., of William Rouse.

In my next article I shall use Columbia as a basis for examining some problems in the social planning of New Towns. The example of Reston lends itself better to a discussion of land planning and design approaches. With respect to the "Year 2000" plan, Reston is slightly off one of the corridors proposed for intense development and is located in a green-wedge area. Here R. E. Simon assembled 7,180 acres of beautiful wooded land for $1,900 an acre (considered rather high by other developers). Of this land, 1,600 acres have been set aside for parks and recreational use; the remaining area will accommodate 75,000 people at the relatively low density of fourteen per acre. The novel concept of Reston is to provide recreation within the town area. The home owner or apartment dweller will, so to speak, live in his own country club. This eliminates 20 per cent of vehicle trips, and the provision of employment within the town area will reduce essential movement still further. Each of Reston's seven vil-

Reston, Virginia. This nursery-kindergarten is being conducted on a rooftop playground. (William Graham—Conklin and Rossant, architects)

lages will have a distinct character, developed from a hobby or a topographical feature. The first village has its lake; new centers are planned around a golf course, a riding stable, a natural amphitheatre, a hill and a valley. Such organization will give identity to each village but the juxtaposition of villages needs an additional unifying concept. Therefore, high-density housing will not be concentrated in one area, but will form "sinews," continuous linear patterns connecting the nodal villages. These sinews will provide an overall structure for the town, and offer visual guidance. One major discontinuity will remain, since the Dulles Airport access highway cuts Reston in half; it will be difficult to tie the segments together.

A variation of the "sinew" concept is proposed

Reston, Virginia. Washington Plaza is one of the main shopping areas, and townhouses are built on top of the stores. (Conklin and Rossant, architects)

by the same architects for Germantown, where high-density housing will form a ring around central open spaces that contain a community campus and research complex for education and employment. According to Conklin, Reston will provide housing for all income levels, but thus far the population is fairly homogeneous, since houses are priced between $22,700 and $47,500. This deprives the town of some of the dynamism provided by the tension and contrast of a greater income spread. Simon now awaits FHA approval to lower mortgage rates and broaden his market. Meanwhile, tourist traffic contributes to the liveliness of the center and helps to support the shops and such extras as the art gallery.

Reston's land planning offers so many excellent ideas that one wishes the developer and town full success, and is reluctant to criticize any part of it. Yet I find some aspects of the design disappointing. The architecture has been praised as boldly adventurous; to my regret, I find it timid, quaint and eclectic. . . . The cluster principle is old hat and there is here nothing to compare with the convincing novelty of the best recent foreign housing schemes —the Swiss terrace housing with cooperative units overlapping one another, the tightly packed patio houses of Halen, or the—admittedly expensive— experimental houses being built for the "Expo" in Montreal. On the defensive, Conklin said that "the range of freedom of planners and designers, although real, is more limited by the nature of society than is usually admitted." Does this mean that our society yearns for eclectic urban design? Does it mean that Reston offers the most adventurous housing that the American market will tolerate? I hope that the subdivision entrepreneurs can be proved wrong and that in subsequent New Towns the range of architectural freedom will extend to housing that projects the future to complement housing that conjures up the past.

Footnotes

Footnotes

THE PROBLEM AND THE CHALLENGE

1. Quoted in Morris Duane, "Behind the Renaissance," *Saturday Review,* vol. 49, no. 2, January 8, 1966, p. 48.
2. Whitney Young, Jr., "We Are in Terrible Danger," *The City in Crisis* (A. Philip Randolph Educational Fund, 1967), p. 27.
3. William Bridgewater and Seymour Kurtz, eds., *The Columbia Encyclopedia* (3rd ed.; New York: Columbia University Press, 1963), p. 422.
4. Lewis Mumford, *The Culture of Cities* (New York: Harcourt, Brace and Company, 1938).
5. Max Lerner, *America as a Civilization* (New York: Simon and Schuster, 1957), p. 157.
6. Lewis Mumford, *op. cit.,* p. 5.
7. *Ibid.*
8. Constance Green, *The Rise of Urban America* (New York: Harper & Row, 1965), p. 47.
9. Will Careton, *City Ballads* (New York: Harper and Bros., 1886), p. 15.
10. Max Lerner, *op. cit.,* p. 158.
11. *Ibid.,* pp. 158–159.
12. *Ibid.*
13. Jean Gottman, *Megalopolis* (New York: The Twentieth Century Fund, 1961), p. 6.

14. Ralph Lazarus, "Surviving the Age of the City," *Saturday Review,* vol. 49, no. 2, January 8, 1966, p. 44.

15. Irving Kirtsol, "It's Not a Bad Crisis to Live In," *The New York Times Magazine,* January 22, 1967, p. 23.

16. Max Lerner, *op. cit.,* p. 164.

17. Robert C. Weaver, *The Urban Complex* (New York: Doubleday Anchor Books, 1966), p. 281.

18. See Jean Gottman, *op. cit.,* chaps. 9 and 11.

Index

Index

Advertising, 95-98
Air transportation, 106, 108
Albany, New York, 32
Algeria, 72
American Broadcasting Company (ABC), 95
Aristotle, 15, 16, 63
Athens, Greece, 27
Automobile, 22, 36, 41, 48, 57, 85, 101, 102, 165-66

Babylon, 131-34
Baltimore, Maryland, 32, 171-72
  Enoch Pratt Free Library, 98
Barclay, Dorothy, 73-78
Battery Park City (New York City), (fig.) 59, (fig.) 123
Birth rate, 34
Book publishing, 98
Boston, Massachusetts, 80, 94, 151
  Eutaw Place, 114
  North End, 114
  South End, 114
Brasilia, Brazil, 163-67
Brooklyn (New York City), 45
Bryan Woods neighborhood center (Columbia, Maryland), (fig.) 64

Buffalo, New York, 32, 80, 82
Bureau of the Census, 44
Burlington, Vermont, 82
Buses, 106

California. See Los Angeles; San Francisco
Canada, 70, 74
Canal Street (New Orleans), 150, 152
Columbia Broadcasting System (CBS), 95
Census, 44, 69, 79
Chicago, Illinois, 44, 51, 114, 157
  Chicago River, 142, 147
  early history, 141-48
  fire of 1871, 85-86, 151
  growth, 19, 29, 40, 143, 147
  Highland Park, 51
  immigration, 80, 82
  Lake Michigan, 142
  Loop, 142
  railroad terminal, 32, 143
  Slab Town, 142, 143
  Trenton Hotel, 143, 146
Chicago River, 142, 147
China, 170
Chinatown (New York City), 45
Chinatown (San Francisco), 86

Cincinnati, Ohio, 147
Cities
  attraction, 34, 38-39
  and community, 24-27
  cost of living, 48
  definition, 17-24, 69-72
  early American, 30-33, 34
  future, 61-66
  goals, 123-30
  good life in, 15-16, 30,
    33, 51, 61, 62, 128-29
  growth, (fig.) 16, 19-22,
    28-29, 32, 34-39, 60,
    100, 107
  health in, 73-74
  human dimension, 125-30
  influence of, 45
  lack of planning, 57-58
  measurements in, 126-28
  neighborhoods, 111-30
  personal relationships, 26-
    27
  planning, 58-61
  reasons for leaving, 47-51
  rich in, 22, 52-53, 101
  safety in, 124, 127
  services, 26, 48, 53, 54,
    88-89
  and suburbs, 61-62
  technological changes, 28-
    29, 61
  universal, 121-30
  See also specific cities and
    subjects
Cleveland, Ohio, 32, 54, 80
Columbia, Maryland, (fig.)
  64, 172
Columbia, North Carolina,
  32
Communication, 29, 126, 128
Community
  city as, 24-27
  early, 28-29
  rural areas, 26, 27, 33
Community Research, Inc.,
  172
Commuting, 101, 127. See
  also Traffic congestion;
  Transportation
Congo, 71
Connecticut, 44. See also
  New Haven
Cortes, Hernando, 135-40
Cost of living, 48, 52
Cotton Exchange (New Or-
  leans), 151
Crime, 48, 54, 58, 61, 74,
  88-89
Czechoslovakia, 72

Delinquency, 54, 112
Denmark, 70
Detroit, Michigan, 29, 32, 40,
  44, 54, 80
Dominican Republic, 72
Dos Passos, John, 163-67
Doxiadis, C. A., 121-30, 171
Dulles Airport approach
  highway, 173

East St. Louis, Illinois, 85
Eastern seaboard. See Met-
  ropolitan areas
Eckardt, Wolf von, 90-99
Educational and cultural in-
  stitutions, 98
Enoch Pratt Free Library
  (Baltimore, Maryland),
  98
Entopia, 123-30
Erie Canal, 32
Euphrates River, 133
European cities, 28, 29, 170
Eutaw Place (Boston), 114

"Expo," Montreal (Quebec), 175
Exurbanization, 41, 44

Fall line, 31-32
Federal Bureau of Investigation (F.B.I.), 74
Federal government, 91, 94
Federal Housing Authority (FHA), 174
Federal Reserve Board, 94
Finland, 70
Fire department, 26, 48, 56, 88-89
Foundations, 98
France, 170
French quarter (New Orleans), (fig.) 154-55, 156
Future of cities, 61-66, 123-30

Galantay, Ervin, 168-76
"Garden City," 170
Geographic factors, 30-32
Germantown, 172, 174
Ghana, 70
Government
  cities, 17, 18-19, 28, 44, 61
  Federal, 91, 94
  metropolitan areas, 44, 61, 62, 63
Great Britain, 72, 170
Great Neck (New York), 51
Greece, 27, 70
Greenwich Village (New York City), (fig.) 33
Growth of cities, (fig.) 16, 29, 32, 60, 107
  birth rate, 34
  communication, 29
  geographic factors, 30-32
  industrial progress, 36-38

migration, 34-36, 37
railroads, 32
transportation, 19-22, 29
women, 38-39

Harvard University, 98
Herodotus, 131-34
Highland Park (Chicago), 51
Highways, 106-07, 173
Hippodamus of Miletus, 171
Hiroshima, 160
Howard, Ebenezer, 117 n., 170, 171
Hudson River, 30
Human dimension of cities, 125-30

Illinois. See Chicago; East St. Louis
Immigration, 34, (fig.) 37, 38, 40, 45, 79, 80-83, 88
India, 70
Industrial progress, 36-38
In-migration, 34, 46, 53
Irish immigration, 38, 80, 82, 88
Irvine Ranch, California, 171
Is, 132
Isaacs, Reginald, 117-18, 119

Jacobs, Jane, 111-20
Japan, 72
Jews, (fig.) 37, 38, 45, 82
Jones, Emrys, 69-72

Kansas City, Missouri, 29

Labor force, 37-38
Lake Anne Plaza (Reston, Virginia), 168
Lake Michigan, 142

Las Vegas, Nevada, 29
L'Enfant, Pierre Charles, 59
Lerner, Max, 29, 38-39
Libraries, 96, 98
Little Italy (New York City), 45
London, England, 19
Loop (Chicago), 142
Los Angeles, California, 29, (fig.) 57, 80
Lower East Side (New York City), (fig.) 18, (fig.) 37

McKelvey, Blake, 79-83
Madison Avenue (New York City), 95
Manhattan (New York City), 59. See also New York City
Maraini, Fosco, 157-62
Maryland. See Baltimore; Columbia
Massachusetts. See Boston
Medieval cities, 28, 30
Megalopolis. See Metropolitan areas
Metropolitan areas
  advertising, 95-98
  book publishing, 98
  California seaboard, 91
  center of, 52, 61, 92-95, 98
  definition, 44
  eastern seaboard, 40, 90-91, 94-96, 97-99
  educational and cultural institutions, (fig.) 96, 98
  governments, 61, 91, 94
  Megalopolis, 90-98
  Midwest, 91
  people of, 98-99
  public relations, 98
  slums, 99

Metropolitan Museum of Art (New York City), 98
Mexico City, Mexico, 135-40
Miami, Florida, 29
Michigan. See Detroit
Middle class, 22, 41, 44, 47-52, 53, 54-56
Migrant farm workers, (fig.) 35
Migration to cities, 34, 37-38, 40. See also Immigration; In-migration
Milwaukee, Wisconsin, 54, 80, 82
Minneapolis, Minnesota, 80
Minnesota. See Minneapolis
Mississippi River, 30
Missouri. See Kansas City; St. Louis
Montgomery Village, 172
Montreal, Quebec (Canada), 175
Morningside Heights (New York City), 114-15
Mumford, Lewis, 28

Nagasaki, 160
Nassau County (New York), 40-41
National Broadcasting Company (NBC), 95
Negroes, 38, 46, (fig.) 47, 53, 54, 101
Neighborhoods
  housing in, 111-12
  ideal, 115-16, 117
  mobility, 117-18
  planning, 116, 117
  poverty areas, 114
  schools, 114, 117

self-management, 115, 118-19
stability, 119-20
in towns, 116-17, 118, 120
universal, 121-30
New England, 29
New Haven, Connecticut, 58
New Jersey, 44. *See also* Newark; Trenton
New Orleans, Louisiana, 30, 80
Canal Street, 150, 152
Cotton Exchange, 151
in 1880's, 149-56
French quarter, *(fig.)* 154-55, 156
Spanish Fort, 152
West End, 152
New Towns
ancient, 170
Columbia, Maryland, *(fig.)* 64, 172
European, 170
Germantown, 172, 174
Irvine Ranch, California, 171
Montgomery Village, 172
proposed, 108
Reston, Virginia, 62, 168-76
United States, 170, 171
New York City, New York, *(fig.)* 39, 41, 152
Battery Park City, *(fig.)* 59, *(fig.)* 123
Brooklyn, 45
Chinatown, 45
Downtown, *(fig.)* 92-93
Erie Canal, 32
financial and economic center, 94, 95
growth, 19, 32
immigration, 38, 82, 88

Little Italy, 45
lower Broadway, 85
Lower East Side, *(fig.)* 18, *(fig.)* 37
Madison Avenue, 95
Manhattan, 59
mass communication center, 95-96
Metropolitan Museum of Art, 98
Morningside Heights, 114-15
New York Philharmonic, 98
New York Public Library, *(fig.)* 96
Times Square, *(fig.)* 86, 95
transportation, 84-85
Upper West Side, 114 n.
Wall Street, 95
West Greenwich Village, 114
New York Metropolitan Region, 44
New York Philharmonic, 98
New York Public Library, *(fig.)* 96
New York State, 73. *See also* Albany; Buffalo; New York City; Poughkeepsie
Newark, New Jersey, 44, 54
Niebuhr, Reinhold, 114
Niemeyer, Oscar, 164
Ninus, 131
North Carolina. *See* Columbia; Raleigh
North End (Boston), 114

Off-street parking, 102
Ohio. *See* Cincinnati; Cleveland

Ohio River, 30

Owen, Wilfred, 100-10

Palace Hotel (Brasilia), 163

Paper Bag Players, Inc., *(fig.)* 109

Penn, William, 58, 59

Pennsylvania. *See* Philadelphia; Pittsburgh

Philadelphia Art Museum, 98

Philadelphia, Pennsylvania, 32, 44, 58-59, *(fig.)* 60, 94

  Philadelphia Art Museum, 98

Pittsburgh, Pennsylvania, 29, 30, 112

Planning

  lack of, 57-58

  Manhattan, New York, 59

  neighborhoods, 116, 117

  New Haven, Connecticut, 58

  Philadelphia, Pennsylvania, 58-59, *(fig.)* 60

  suburbs, 60

  urban renewal, 61

  Washington, D.C., 59, 94

  zoning, 60, 116

Plato, 63

Police department, 26, 48, 54, 56, 88, *(fig.)* 103

Pollution, 47, 58, 88, 89, 99, 101

Population pressure, 125

Potomac River, 30, 94

Poughkeepsie, New York, *(fig.)* 63

Pride, Inc., *(fig.)* 50

Princeton University, 98

Public relations, 98

Puerto Ricans, 38, 46, 53, 54

Pullman, George M., 146

Queen Elizabeth I, 19

Race riots, 54

Radio, 95

Railroads, 32, 143

Raleigh, North Carolina, 32

Recreation, 48, 52, *(fig.)* 104

Residential patterns, 45

Restaurants, *(fig.)* 51

Reston, Virginia, 62, *(fig.)* 65, 168-76

  Dulles Airport access highway, 173

  Lake Anne Plaza, 168

  Washington Plaza, *(fig.)* 174

Revolutionary War, 36, 59

Rich (in cities), 22, 52-53, 101

Riesman, David, 74

Rio Doce Company, 166-67

Riots, 16, 54, 101

Rivers, 30-31, 133, 142

Rogers, Taliaferro, Kostritski & Lamb, 172

Rome, Italy, 27, *(fig.)* 71, 170

Rouse, William, 172

Rumania, 72

Rural areas

  birth rate, 34

  children, 76

  communities in, 26, 27, 33

  crime, 74

  good life in, 33

  life style, 76

  migrant farm workers, *(fig.)* 35

movement to cities, 34-36
population, 40
Russell, O. D., 158 n.

Safety in cities, 124, 127
St. Louis, Missouri, 30-31,
32, 80
San Francisco, California,
(fig.) 21, 40, 44
Chinatown, 86
fire of 1906, 86
Gold Rush of 1849, 29
immigration, 80
Sanitation, 48, (fig.) 50, 56
Schools, 48, 52, 53, 54, (fig.)
55-56, 101, 112, 114,
117, 123
Securities and Exchange
Commission, 94
Services
cities, 26, 48, 53, 54, 88-
89
New Towns, 62
suburbs, 55
Shaker Heights (Cleveland),
51
Simon, R. E., 170, 172, 174
Slab Town, 142, 143
Slums
crime, 48
ghettos as, 46, (fig.) 47
growth, 48, 58, 61, 99
housing in, 53, 85, 100-01
South End (Boston), 114
South Philadelphia, Pennsyl-
vania, 85
Spanish Fort (New Orleans),
152
Staggered working hours,
103-05
Steam locomotive, 19-20
Streetcar, 20-22, 36, 57

Suburbs, 40-44, 47, 51-52,
54-56, 61-62, 76-78
Subway, 22, 36, 47, 48, 54,
57, 101
Sweden, 70, 170

Taxes, 48, 52, 53, 54, 55
Telephone, 152
Television, 95, 128
Tenochtitlán (Mexico), 135-
40
Times Square (New York
City), (fig.) 86, 95
Tokyo, Japan, 157-62
Towns, 69-72, 74, 116-17,
118, 120
Toynbee, Arnold J., 158
Traffic congestion, 54, (fig.)
57, 58, 99, 101
Transportation
air, 106, 108
automobile, 22, 36, 41, 106
in cities, 19-22, 29, 36, 47,
48, 54, 57, 84-85, 99,
101-02, 106, 126, 128
railroads, 32, 106
Tremont Hotel (Chicago),
143, 146
Trenton, New Jersey, 32
Triangle of the Three Powers
(Brasilia), 164
Trolley lines. See Streetcars
Tunisia, 72
Turkey, 72
Twain, Mark, 149-56

United Arab Republic, 72
United Kingdom, 72
United States, 70, 85, 170.
See also specific states
and cities
Universal city, 121-30

Upper West Side (New York
    City), 114 n.
Urban population, 40
Urban renewal, 61, 102-10
Urban sprawl, 44, 107
Urbanization
    future of, 125
    rural areas, 40
    suburbs, 40-44, 46
    urban sprawl, 44, 107
USSR, 170

Venezuela, 70
Vergennes, Vermont, 18
Vernon, Raymond, 84-89

Wall Street (New York
    City), 95
Warner, Charles Dudley, 147
Washington, D.C., 30, 44,
    59, 94
    "Year 2000" plan, 171-72
Washington-Baltimore conur-
    bation, 171-72

Washington Plaza (Reston,
    Virginia), *(fig.)* 174
Waterfalls. *See* Fall line
Welfare, 54
West End (New Orleans),
    152
West Greenwich Village
    (New York City), 114
Westchester County (New
    York), 40-41
Whittlesey, Conklin and Ros-
    sant, 172, 174, 175
Wisconsin. *See* Milwaukee
Women, 38-39
Woodward, William E., 141-
    48

Yale University, 58, 98
"Year 2000" plan (Wash-
    ington, D.C.), 171-72

Zoning, 60, 116

GENERAL EDITOR

Gerald Leinwand is Professor of Education and Chairman of the Department of Education at the Bernard M. Baruch College of the City University of New York. Dr. Leinwand received his B.A., M.S., and Ph D. degrees from New York University and an M.A. from Columbia University. In addition to numerous magazine articles, he is the author of *The Pageant of World History, The American Constitution: A Tutor-Text,* and a college text *Teaching History and the Social Studies in Secondary Schools.*

100